CREATING
How and Why Governors and
the CAPACITY
Legislatures Are Opening a
for CHANGE
New-Schools Sector in Public Education

TED KOLDERIE

EDUCATION WEEK PRESS

ISBN 0-9674795-3-3

To order copies of this book,

Telephone: (800) 445-8250

Fax: (301) 280-3250

E-mail: capacity@epe.org

Or write: Education Week Press
6935 Arlington Road, Suite 100
Bethesda, MD 20814.

Subscriptions to *Education Week* are available by calling (800) 728-2790.

Visit us on the Web at edweek.org.

To contact the author, visit www.EducationEvolving.org, or call (651) 644-6115.

Also from the EDUCATION WEEK PRESS:

Living the Legacy: *Education Week* Marks the 50th Anniversary
of the *Brown v. Board of Education of Topeka* Decision

Building Bridges With the Press: A Guide for Educators

Miles To Go ... Reflections on Mid-Course Corrections For Standards-Based Reform

Photo Credit: Cover photo courtesy of Tom Olmscheid, Minnesota House of Representatives

TABLE OF CONTENTS

■ ■ ■ ■ ■ ■

Preface

About 1980 I began to write occasional memos about what I then thought of as "public services redesign". These grew out of work in Minnesota on general questions about the organization of the public sector; work that had its roots in the urban troubles of the 1960s and the dramatic loss of confidence in public institutions in the 1970s. I was involved in a project known as Public Service Options, trying along with others around the country to rethink some of the basic concepts of government's role.

Into the early 1980s this work did not significantly involve public education. The schools had not at that point been caught up in the critical reappraisal being directed at urban renewal, public housing, welfare, health care and other social service programs. But with the release of *A Nation At Risk* in 1983 this changed, and education—the schools—joined the list of institutions under review as to their performance, responsiveness and cost.

So by the mid-'80s the memos from my project—then located at the Humphrey Institute, the school of public affairs at the University of Minnesota—were beginning to explore questions about change and improvement in K-12 education. There was a rich discussion in Minnesota about this, resulting partly from Jim Kelly's arrival as president of Spring Hill Center and his ability to bring into its conferences people from the network he had developed during his years with the education program of the Ford Foundation. Gov. Al Quie had commissioned work on education policy in 1982, Joe Nathan was stimulating a new discussion about student choice in public education, the Citizens League was working on these questions and by 1983 Berman/Weiler was under way with its study for the Minnesota Business Partnership.

Some of the memos were notes of discussions, some were interviews with national experts here for conferences at Spring Hill or for annual meetings of the National Education Association, the Association of Alternative Educators and other groups. Some were my own effort to think through the problems of this institution and what might be done about them. In these days before websites and email I printed and mailed the memos to a gradually-lengthening list of persons. I was encouraged to find they were being read. Twice, I think, someone called to ask me for a clean copy of one memo or another, saying "The one I have has been copied so many times it won't copy any more".

I mention all this, I suppose, because some will ask whether a book written-largely in the Minnesota context will prove useful—and interesting—to policymakers in other states and to others in the national discussion. This is a small state and—as people do quite often point out—not a typical state. We admire what Minnesota can do, they will say, but of course that has no meaning for us.

It does seem to make sense for the examples and the stories to be drawn from within a state, since the state is the critical arena for education policymaking. It seems to me, too, that Minnesota's policy discussion is a reasonable one from which to draw examples. The system-arrangements in public education and the institutional behaviors that result, and the issues these present, are broadly similar across the states. And for 30 years policy developments in Minnesota have been contributing significantly to the national discussion: the 1971 re-equalization of education finance, the tuition-tax-deduction which produced the *Mueller* v. *Allen* decision, the post-secondary option in 1985, inter-district open enrollment in 1988, the chartering law in 1991, the tax credit in 1996, the state's assumption of district operating cost in 2001 and most recently the idea of teacher professional ownership. A number of these have made their way through law and policy into the K-12 system-arrangements in other states and into national policy, and continue to be actively discussed.

I have to hope that those operating the institution will not put down a book from a non-educator; will not say, as insiders often do, that no one can understand an institution who has not been involved in running it. That might not be true. The problems of system design, especially, are sometimes understood more clearly and acted on more effectively by people outside. Those inside the institution may not be the most insightful, or the most candid, or the best positioned or most motivated to act. On this kind of system problem the knowledge of academic research about learning and the management experience of operators might not be essential. It might be better, actually, for the analysis and the proposals to come from someone whose experience has been largely with state policymakers in the redesign of large public systems.

To some readers this book will sound critical of 'public education'. So it is important to be clear at the start what—and who—is being criticized, and not, and why.

We all recognize the accomplishments of this institution. In a decentralized and democratic process people in local communities began more than 150 years ago to create public schools to educate and train their children. Over the years, with help from the state, the districts' administration was professionalized, the number of districts was cut by 80 per cent in the 1930s and '40s, new schools were built to handle the growth in enrollment after 1945. Even if with difficulty, the institution adapted to children with handicaps, to racial integration and to collective bargaining.

Public education also has weaknesses: serious inequities and much difficulty with change. Like many things in life the institution is successful and unsuccessful, good and bad, at the same time. This book deals mainly with its inadequacies because these are now the issue; a serious problem for the country, complicating its effort to upgrade the knowledge and skills of its people. Praising the past would not help solve the present problem.

The people who work in K-12 are not to be criticized for the weaknesses of the institution. I remember saying this at a meeting at the Harvard Graduate School of Education in 1993; telling a group of state legislators "It's your fault", the state's fault. The people in K-12 cannot change their institution; only the legislature can change it.[1] The people in the institution can be criticized, however, when they fail to point out its weaknesses and when they resist as the legislatures try to fix its problems. This is the ethical issue I raise in Chapter 12.

If this book proves useful it will be due to all I have learned from those who know education and education policy and from those who know politics and state policymaking. I remain a kind of journalist, who depends on his sources for his knowledge and his understanding of fields in which he is inexpert himself. Many people have been enormously helpful; especially my colleagues in Education/ Evolving and especially Joe Graba, who saw clearly before the rest of us, from his experience both in public education and in politics, that the answers did not lie in trying to change the schools we have. I am responsible of course for the analysis and for the conclusions you see here.

The analysis and discussion is important: Ideas are important. But the changes now under way are due really to the efforts of the legislators and governors in so many states who have brought a new sector of public education into law against determined opposition at a time when practically no support for this idea was visible in public opinion. And to those teachers and parents and others who moved so quickly as the new laws appeared to do what so many would have said could not be done: to start and run new public schools for children failing—or being failed—in traditional schools.

We are only beginning to appreciate the remarkable success of both, in opening up this new and innovative sector of public education.

Ted Kolderie

September 2004

---

[1]See Chapter 10.

THE CURRENT THEORY OF ACTION CONTAINS A CRITICAL FLAW

This country is trying hard to improve its public education but not thinking clearly enough about how, realistically, to get that done.

By introducing standards and measurement and consequences we have directed, commanded, the schools to improve. With its legislation in 2002 the national government is talking tough about accountability. But talking tough does not by itself make things happen: It is not usually productive to order people to do what in truth they cannot do. We need to think more clearly about the institution being able to do what it is being ordered to do.

The national discussion about improvement—so largely about standards and leadership and resources—tends to see as a problem of changing organizations what is in fact a problem of changing the institution. At bottom the problem is not one of organizational capacity. The problem is one of institutional capacity. The current arrangement of K-12 public education neither makes it possible to transform the existing districts and schools into something very different, nor significantly encourages the appearance of new organizations able to do better. We have a system problem.

It may seem surprising that we have failed so far to get to the heart of this question about the capacity to improve. Clearly anyone giving an order should want the other party to be able to comply. But the discussion has taken the traditional institutional arrangement as a given, and has gone directly to questions about 'improving the capacity' of districts and of schools and about enhancing the instructional skills of teachers. The assumption is that the clarity and coherence provided by new curricular frameworks, stronger leadership, better training, tougher accountability and richer financing will overcome whatever disincentives to change and performance are inherent in the present arrangement of K-12 education as essentially a regulated public utility. It is assumed these organizational improvements will be made, can be made.

This strategy began to emerge in the early '90s: national action to stimulate state action to stimulate district action to improve schooling. It was visible in national legislation in 1994. Then in the late '90s developments in national politics cleared the way for more dramatic steps. After 15 years of little progress, the public and its political leaders were in a mood to get tough with the organizations, to 'make 'em' improve.

In national politics education had long been understood to be "a Democratic issue": Money was the measure of commitment (and presumably the key to success) and Democrats would always top what Republicans were willing to spend. But by 2000, with education the public's number-one concern, the Republicans saw that to win the presidency they had to capture that 'issue'. The strategy was to try to make accountability trump money. And they did it. Once in office the new administration, using the national government's (seven per cent) contribution to K-12 finance as the lever, moved immediately to persuade Congress to enact the president's campaign slogan about "leaving no child behind". As it passed into law early in 2002 the idea was to require that all kids score well on standardized tests and to threaten either the kids or the schools with sanctions should they fail.

We do not know that this can be done. Pretty clearly it never has been done, in this country at least. No one demonstrated following A Nation at Risk in 1983 that it could be done. It was simply assumed that poor schools could and would be turned into good schools like caterpillars transformed into butterflies, with poor students turned into good students. There was no other concept in the policy thinking. The language of the discussion makes this clear: It is all about renewing, reforming, reinventing, restructuring, revitalizing, remodeling, reengineering, reconstituting; endlessly, 're-', 're-', 're-'. There has been little serious consideration that the absence of accountability and the ineffectiveness of leadership and the chronic demands for more revenue and the deficiencies in teacher practice are the result of a fundamental incapacity in the institutional arrangements.

This is the central issue now for policy: whether it is realistic to assume that law and regulation and exhortation can overcome the constraints of faulty system design. Even if conceivably they might, the uncertainty makes such an assumption clearly a risk. Remember: The bar is set very high. We are talking seriously about educating all students to high standards. This asks a lot of the organizations we have. It may be that within the present arrangements the job cannot be done.

In a conversation in the spring of 2003 I put the concern about this risk to a leading proponent of standards-based systemic reform. He thought a moment. "It is a one-bet strategy", he said.

A one-bet strategy is always a risk. It is a serious risk to be taking on something as important to the nation and to its people as public education. And it is not a prudent risk to be taking since it is not a necessary risk to be taking: We do not have to limit ourselves to trying to get existing districts to improve existing schools. We can be moving at the same time to create the different and better schools new.

Because it is not a necessary risk it is not an acceptable risk for policy leadership to be taking, with other people's children. It is troubling that the public is being given so little sense of the risk that the current strategy might not succeed.

Success will require changing the old arrangements

Almost certainly it was necessary politically for those who shaped the current national strategy to accept the existing institutional arrangements. If 'systemic reform' had not been seen to accept this framework the major players in public education—the superintendents, boards and teacher unions—would not have listened. So proponents had to assume that districts, told what standards to meet and held accountable for results, could and would change and improve the schools they own and run; had to bet all the chips on the districts getting us the schools we need by changing the schools we have.

A theory is a statement that if we do X then Y will result. It is critical that the theory be valid; that Y in fact result when X is done. The concern rising from the experience so far is that—as now arranged—the institution will not produce the results we want, even when directed to do so.

The problem, the critical flaw in the current theory, is the acceptance of those existing arrangements. The prevailing theory sets the question incorrectly. It asks whether changing structure improves 'instruction', and to that question answers, No. So far, fair enough. Clearly what will improve learning will be improvements in what teachers and students do, and in the methods and materials they use. Still, structure matters. The correct question, the important question, the practical question for policymakers, is: Within what structure, under what arrangements, is this effort to 'improve instruction' likely to be more succesful?

The prevailing theory does not really defend the existing arrangement; simply accepts it. But this regulated-public-utility arrangement has made public education an inert institution, lacking the capacity to do what we now need it to do. As a result the process of improvement has become largely an effort to push improvement into the inert institution. We have been treating public education like a patient in intensive care, supported by casts and pulleys, hooked up with tubes and wires flowing in nourishment and stimulus from the outside. We have been trying to do for the organizations the good things they did not do for themselves.

This is basically ridiculous as a strategy. Why, if we want the districts to change, would we leave in place the constraints that make it so difficult for them to change?

Normally we arrange our institutions to be self-improving institutions, so the organizations within them become self-improving organizations. This means structuring the institutions so their organizations will do, themselves, the good things that need to be done: set standards, measure performance, impose consequences, control costs, improve practices, prepare leadership and innovate with new technology. And will do these things on their own initiative, in their own interest and from their own resources.

About 1984 William Andres, then just retired as CEO of Dayton-Hudson Corporation, was asked by the governor to head a task force on productivity in Minnesota state government. Andres asked others more familiar with the public sector: "Is productivity something you do, or something that happens if you do the fundamentals right?" If you paused to think he would explain: "I was in retailing. In retailing turnover is very important: Stores that turn over their inventory rapidly are more profitable. Every so often a store manager tries to 'do' turnover, and quickly that store isn't profitable any more. So in our company we decided a long time ago that turnover is something that happens, and we concentrate on doing the fundamentals right."

That puts much in perspective about the strategy for education. We are trying to 'do improvement' when we should be working to get the fundamentals right. We should be arranging this institution so its organizations make and are able to make, themselves, the changes and improvements needed. We should be restructuring the K-12 institution so it too becomes a self-improving institution. This means we cannot take present arrangements as given. The flaw in the theory of action, that confines policy to efforts within present arrangements, will have to be fixed.

We need to think about this now very soon—broadly and carefully and sensibly and above all with realism about the way organizations and institutions behave.

This book is an attempt to do that. The solution will be difficult to implement but is essentially simple. It is to restructure the K-12 institution to make it possible for new schools to appear; for different and better schools gradually to take the place of low-performing schools—while at the same helping the districts to do what they can to improve the schools they run. This 'two-bet' strategy will hedge against the likelihood that an effort confined to paying, exhorting and commanding the districts to improve will not succeed.

In the 1990s governors and legislatures, following the old rule about always changing a losing game, began to enact laws creating a new 'open sector' in public education, partly inside but substantially outside the district framework. Moving beyond the district required them to withdraw the exclusive franchise that the old public-utility arrangement gave the local board to offer public education. It required being open to the idea that more than one organization can offer public education in the community.

This book describes that new state effort. It will say something about the need for the new schools to be different from the schools that exist today, to have any real chance of educating the students now not learning well in traditional schooling. But as the photo on the cover should suggest, this is not really another book about better schools and better learning. It will not go into questions about learning as an educator would. It is about strategy, about method; is mainly about how to arrange the K-12 institution so it will provide reasons and opportunities for those who are educators to develop and sustain a diversity of quality schools.

Part One explains what it is about the traditional arrangement that makes the K-12 institution inert, that constrains change. Part Two explains what changes will be required in the system for K-12 to become a self-improving institution. Part Three explains what specifically state policy leadership will need to do, and how it can deal with the arguments thrown up against system change. Part Four then asks how quickly the changes can get made and explains who specifically will need to do what specifically.

Change will not be easy. The interests within K-12 will not want to see their institution re-arranged. For understandable reasons they will try as they usually do to hold policy to incremental changes within existing arrangements. But others, outside the institution, have a different interest. It is their children that are at risk, their nation that is still very much at risk.

These others outside K-12—and the state policy leadership that is their agent— are the primary audience for this book. I do hope, though, there will be some educators, and more than a few, who will read it and who will say: Yes, this is what has to happen; it is time.

PART ONE

HOW EXISTING ARRANGEMENTS OBSTRUCT IMPROVEMENT

Chapter 1

INCENTIVES SHAPE ORGANIZATIONS' BEHAVIOR

The old agenda has not given much attention to incentives as they affect the organizations in K-12. Essentially in trying to fix the schools the effort has been to push districts to do things they have neither reasons to do nor opportunities to do, confusing what they 'ought to do' with what they have a reason to do.

The strategy of systemic reform reflects a deep conviction that structure, governance, system 'arrangements', do not provide the significant levers for policy. Changing the system, as its advocates often say, does not change teacher practice or improve student learning.

That is true, but not the point. The arrangements in any institution shape what must be done and what can be done. Set well they can work powerfully to help organizations succeed. Set badly they can present a huge obstacle to success. They create the incentives that shape organizations' behavior.

Suppose a nation wanted to increase the revenue available to charities. Someone might suggest that gifts to charity be exempt from tax. Suppose the response was that, no, we don't want to spend time adjusting the structure of the tax laws. We want to work directly to increase giving. Surely most of us would think such an objection passing strange. It is true of course that exempting gifts from taxation does not directly increase the charities' bank balances: The army of 'development officers' working for charities attests to that. But relatively few charities do not value the incentive for giving created by the tax exemption.

So it is not good to diminish the central importance of structure, in any field. And not in K-12 public education. Incentives matter.

Institutions and organizations tend to behave the way they are structured and rewarded to behave, as Walter McClure of the Center for Policy Studies likes to say. If we do not like the way they are behaving it may not make much difference to tell them to do better or to change the way they are led. We will probably do better to change the way they are structured and rewarded. It makes a difference what an organization has a reason to do, or has no reason to do. It makes a difference what an organization has an opportunity to do, or has no opportunity to do.

Those thinking about incentives do often think about incentives for individuals. It may matter more how incentives are structured for organizations: what reasons they have, to act, and what opportunities they have, to act. Organizations have interests. They want to survive and they want to grow. They protect their turf, their jurisdiction. Organizations have personalities; develop their own culture. They can be jealous, proud, stubborn. Organizations like to be well-regarded. There is a strong drive for self-justification. For-profit or non-profit, they want to maximize and protect their revenues. Many, like many individuals, find change stressful; prefer a quiet life. These interests influence the way they respond as situations change and as policy changes. And the organization's incentives shape its members' behavior.

At the first anniversary of the Saturn School in Saint Paul in May 1991 Albert Shanker, then president of the American Federation of Teachers, talked candidly about the importance of incentives.

He'd stressed first the importance of motivating students, of giving students a reason to work hard. Then he turned to the question of motivating educators, of giving educators a reason to change.

"Something has to be at stake," he said. "There is, in other fields: Your organization could fail. People in these fields dislike change too. But they have to do it. We in education don't, because for us nothing is at stake. If our kids do brilliantly nothing particularly good happens. And if we don't push we can count on remaining popular with our colleagues. . . "We have got to deal with this question of consequences for adults", he said. "Educators simply are not going to take the risks of change, against the pressures of everyday popular feelings, unless they have to."

■ ■ ■ ■

Changing incentives changes behavior
State policy leadership does not have to be frustrated by an institution's low performance and by the resistance from its organizations when the state exhorts it to do better. Or by its sometimes straight-out refusal to comply with legislative intent.

Over the years, as Dan Loritz says, Minnesota tried most everything: tried exhorting districts to improve, tried research to show them how to improve, tried giving them money to improve. Nothing much worked. "So we decided we'd try giving 'em a reason". Loritz was effectively education adviser to Gov. Rudy Perpich in the 1980s. It was in the '80s that Minnesota's effort at system-change began to develop.

But a reason to do something is not enough. Giving people a reason to act, without the opportunity to act, produces only frustration. Nor is it effective just to give people the opportunity: Without the reason nothing will happen either. The two go together.

Incentives exist, intended or not. There are always things an institution and its organizations may do and may not do; there are always reasons for them to act or not to act. These incentives become the 'rules of the game' that shape the way the organizations behave. All of us, all the time, see organizations responding—and rationally—to the incentives created by the system in which they exist. And we see policymakers arranging and rearranging the incentives, sometimes purposefully and sometimes inadvertently; sometimes with good results and sometimes with unfortunate results.

Bad things happen where the incentive-structure is badly designed. Where it is well designed, on the other hand, it can work powerfully for the public interest. It is especially important for policymakers to ensure that the incentive-structure is aligned with the objectives they want the institution to accomplish.

In business

Over the years Congress had reshaped the program of insurance intended to protect funds deposited in savings and loan associations. With deposits insured the S&Ls were able to attract funds because their depositors were secure in the knowledge that any losses would be repaid by federal deposit insurance. In the early 1980s the limits on deposit-insurance were raised from $40,000 to $100,000 per account. "Confident that the government would stand behind even the shakiest institutions, savvy investors deposited $100,000—not a penny more—in S&Ls that offered high interest rates. Thus shielded from the discipline of the market, S&Ls made high-risk loans."[1] Many such loans could not be repaid. Ultimately the defaults cost the taxpayers billions. Some of what happened was criminal behavior, and some people did go to jail. But the real culprit was the incentive created by the deposit insurance.

More recently executives in fast-growing electronics industries began to take their compensation in the form of options to buy company stock at a defined price. This gave them a reason to increase the market price of the stock so they could sell high what they had bought low. This in turn gave them a reason to influence the company's accounting to show 'results' that would drive the share price higher; gave them "a perverse incentive to inflate earnings", as the chairman of the Federal Reserve put it. An effort by the Securities and Exchange Commission to make

---

[1]*Wall Street Journal* March 14, 2002

options chargeable as an expense had been blocked in Congress, leaving in place the opportunities that in time drew executives, accountants and auditors from deception into fraud. Prosecutions are still under way and the country is still working its way out of the problem. Now the regulators are trying again to require options to be reported as compensation expense.

In health insurance

Until the 1930s families paid the hospital and doctor as they paid anyone else who did them a service. But in the depression too many families could not pay. Hospitals were in financial trouble. So the payment system began to be restructured.

First came prepayment: the beginning of what we now call 'health insurance'. This provided a way for families to pay something regularly toward the cost of hospital and doctor bills when they needed care. After 1945 came the idea that some third party ought to make those prepayments for you. Labor unions bargained this into contracts. It was a benefit, not taxable, so unions had a reason to take compensation increases in this form. Employers' willingness gave them the opportunity. So the practice spread rapidly. In 1967, with Medicare, the federal government became a third-party payor for persons over 65.

This restructuring of health-care finance had dramatic effects. Powerful incentives were at work; old reasons combined with new opportunities. Patients wanted the best care, doctors wanted to provide the best treatment (and to earn fees), hospitals wanted to have the best facilities, technology companies wanted to sell the best equipment. And neither the patient nor the doctor or hospital had to pay directly. The bill was sent to the insurers. The law let insurers recover their costs. So they raised premiums accordingly. Employers then built the higher premium costs into the price of their products. Essentially this cost-pass-through arrangement simply sent doctor and hospital bills to the American economy for payment. By the mid-1970s health-care costs were rising by more than 10 per cent a year and were consuming almost 14 per cent of gross domestic product.

Looking at the situation, Anne and Herman Somers went to the heart of this system-design: "In no other realm of economic life is repayment guaranteed for costs that are neither controlled by competition nor regulated by public authority and in which no incentive for economy can be discerned".[2]

Telling hospitals and doctors that they would be reimbursed for whatever they did was in effect giving them an incentive to do everything; was like a baseball owner telling his players he would pay them by the number of times they swung the bat. It had to be changed. Soon capitation appeared; the idea of giving hospitals and

---

[2]Herman M. and Anne R. Somers, *Medicare and the Hospitals*, Brookings Institution, 1967.

doctors a reason both to constrain use and to keep people healthy. Give them a fixed amount, let them pay the patients' bills, let them keep what they did not need to spend. Provide a choice of plans and the information about hospital and physician 'batting averages' that patients need to make good decisions.

Health-maintenance organizations and other forms of 'managed care' appeared. Much was accomplished. The rate of increase in health-care costs slowed dramatically. But policy probably went too far in reversing the incentives. By the 1980s there were charges that the health plans were scanting care in favor of profits. For 20 years the country has been struggling to find the right balance of incentives, in an intricately complex system. Only recently are policy thinkers coming back to getting the incentives right: identify the high-quality, low-cost clinics and hospitals and arrange the benefits program to flow them patients; essentially what Walter McClure and Paul Ellwood were arguing in the early 1980s.[3]

In education

In the early '80s Florida enacted a program of school-based management for districts. One district gave its schools their money in a lump. The schools paid their own bills for energy and the like. And they could keep for school activities money they did not need to spend. District officials quickly noticed the electric bills beginning to drop. Students and teachers were turning off the lights and the air-conditioning when they left the classroom. This generated money to pay for field trips and other activities. The site-management program had been structured, even if unintentionally, to give the kids and teachers a reason and an opportunity to behave differently. And they responded to the incentive created.[4]

While superintendent in Milwaukee Howard Fuller saw teachers absent too often. The cost of the substitutes at that time fell on the district budget. Fuller restructured the 'substitutes' program to give each school its share of the budget for substitutes, and to make each school pay for its own substitutes (i.e., pay for teacher-absences). Each school could keep what it did not need to spend. As with the energy costs in that Florida school, teacher-absences went down.

Michael Kirst, Stanford University professor and former chair of the California State Board of Education, has long been concerned about students' preparation for college. To him it is a matter of the incentives not being set right. If colleges admit students based partly on grade-point-average (as they do), if students want to get admitted to college (as they do) and if students may choose the courses they take in

---

[3]See Professor Michael Porter's article in the *Harvard Business Review*, June 2004. Also the column by Jeff Madrick in *The New York Times* July 8, 2004.

[4]Related by Larry Pierce, then at the University of Oregon, to a meeting convened by the Northwest Area Foundation in Saint Paul, August 1982.

high school (as they may), then an incentive exists for students in high school to take less-demanding courses in which they can get higher grades.

In county government

Through the 1950s there was growing conflict between Minneapolis and its suburbs. The city and suburban officials were fighting over taxes, roads, parks, welfare; all advocating, not surprisingly, for their own jurisdictional interests. Everyone knew the 1960 census—reflecting the growth of the suburbs – would require a redistricting of the Hennepin County board.

At the time four of the five commissioners came from the city of Minneapolis, one from the suburbs (then still called "rural Hennepin"). There was a strong desire not to recreate in the restructured county board the city/suburban warfare raging at the municipal level. The Citizens League proposed that five new commissioner districts be laid out with one entirely Minneapolis, one entirely suburban and three overlapping the city/suburban boundary. The idea was to give a majority of commissioners a reason to focus on the problems of the county as a whole; to deny these three an opportunity to represent the interest of either Minneapolis or the suburbs. It worked.

In industry

In the early 1900s there were terrible accidents in the steel mills. The companies took the view that accidents were the workers' problem, not the company's problem. Companies spent their money not for safety but to hire lawyers whose job was to deny liability. Then, beginning in 1911 in Washington, states created a new kind of insurance program. Rather than having injured workers sue in the courts the idea was to accept that accidents happen and to create a workers' compensation fund to pay for the medical care and for the lost income of those injured. The money was raised by an assessment on the employers. Companies, knowing they would pay the costs, quickly saw a reason to introduce safety programs in order to reduce their costs—which of course they had always had the opportunity to do. Over the succeeding 20 years the injury rate in the iron and steel industry fell by 90 per cent.[5]

Among nations

Three times between 1870 and 1940 Germany attacked France. In 1950, as Cold War tensions made the United States want to rearm Germany, the fears of Germany recurred in France. Thinking about the problem it seemed to Jean Monnet that the answer was to change the context; to merge the interests of the two nations so that war was unthinkable, impossible. He began by persuading the Schuman government in France to propose the merger of the coal and steel industries of Germany

---

[5]The story is told in Mark Aldrich, *Safety First*, Johns Hopkins Press, 1997.

and France, in an arrangement open to the participation of others. What became the Coal and Steel Community evolved into the Common Market, then into the broader (and still-expanding) European Community. By 2003 it was possible to drive from Lisbon to Vienna without showing a passport or changing your money.

'The system' creates the incentives

Incentives do powerfully shape behavior. They can have good effects or bad effects. So they need to be structured with care. However virtuous the intentions, all efforts to change the way business or health care or education is built need to consider what incentives are being created. It will not do to ask, later, questions like, "Who foresaw that health insurance, which was supposed to help people stay healthy, also would create a disastrous inflation in health-care costs?" Consequences can be foreseen.

An effort to change behavior through incentives rather than through commands, by altering the structure of opportunity and reward for organizations, needs to be added now to the strategy for the improvement of public education. Changing the incentives needs to be our concept of 'changing the system'.

This requires some explanation, because 'system' has quite different meanings for different people.

I once asked an analyst at RAND Corporation what people there mean when they say 'system'. He answered: "A collection of interacting parts". And that is a common notion of 'system'. The aviation system in this sense is United, American, Delta and the other airline companies, the airport authorities, the FAA air traffic control, etc. The communications system is the telephone companies, the radio and television broadcasters, the FCC, the Internet and the World Wide Web and all the companies involved in electronics, the carriers of hard-copy messages like the Postal Service and Federal Express, etc. The financial system is the banks, the investment houses, the mutual funds, their regulators; on and on. In the public sector we talk about the transportation system, meaning the highways and local streets and the organizations that build them, the transit buses and rail lines and the organizations that run them, the private cars and their owner-drivers, etc. All these are collections of interacting parts.

But there's a second definition. 'System' can also mean the principles on which the interacting parts are organized. We're using this second definition when we talk about a socialist system and a market system, or about the difference between a consumer market and a social market. When we talk about the public sector we talk about authoritarian systems and democratic systems; or, on the operating side, about a bureau system and a contract system. These terms describe the principles that govern the collections of interacting parts. The principles differ radically, the variations creating different incentive-structures, different combinations of opportunities and reward.

This book will reserve the term 'system' for the principles on which things are organized, for the rules of the game. When it means the interacting parts themselves it will talk about 'the institution' and the organizations that make it up.[6]

In this definition the incentives exist initially for organizations. It is well to assume that these incentives will then exist for the individuals in the organization. It is dangerous to assume the reverse: that the imperatives felt by the organization will not also be felt by its members. Or to assume that an organization will be able to impose on its members requirements for performance that do not exist for the organization itself.

The incentives created need to be aligned with the mission the institution and the organizations in it have been given to perform. In the K-12 institution at the moment, unfortunately, they are not. This is a critical flaw in the current effort to get the districts to change existing schools.

---

[6]Sports offer a wonderful opportunity to see the system shaping the behavior of the coaches and the teams; to watch the game change as those in charge adjust its rules in response to changing expectations and changing conditions. See for example *From Six-on-Six to Full Court Press; a Century of Iowa Girls' Basketball*, Janice Beran, Iowa State University Press, 1993.

■ ■ ■ ■ ■ ■
Chapter **2**

THE INCENTIVES ARE NOT ALIGNED WITH THE MISSION

When we talk about 'the education system', then, we are talking about the principles on which the K-12 institution is built; the structure of opportunity and reward created for the schools, the districts, the state departments, the teacher unions, the teacher-training colleges, the professional associations.

This is not, again, what the superintendent has in mind when s/he refers to 'the system'. The superintendent means the district organization, "my schools". That will not be our definition here. The district is not the system, nor are all the districts collectively. The districts are parts of the institution.[1]

The principles on which we have built public education differ from those used for most of our institutions. Albert Shanker was noting this difference when he said at the Saturn School that while people in other institutions dislike change too, they "have to" do it and "those of us in education don't".

Most systems are designed to contain a 'have to' that makes change and performance necessary. Business, the nonprofit sector, politics are all built on the principle of open entry. Someone else can come into your field: New businesses and new nonprofits can appear, someone can decide to run for the public office you hold. This means that customers have choices, citizens have choices, voters have choices. People can leave their supplier, their church, their political party and go somewhere else. This creates consequences, good and bad, for organizations. In institutions constructed on these principles an organization can fail. This risk of failure creates an incentive for performance, and so for change.

---

[1] Language is a major problem in the discussion about education policy. Words and concepts are the tools of the policy trade. It is astonishing how careless well-educated and intelligent people can be in their use of terms. At times 'school' is used to mean, literally, school, as in school-based management; at times it means the district, as in school board; at times it means education generally, as in school reform. Sometimes 'school' means the building, sometimes it means what goes on in the building. Usually nobody bothers to define terms. It can be simply chaotic. If a painter came into your house and was as careless with the tools of his trade you'd order him out.

Public education has been different. And the strategy for improvement reflects this difference. Policy has not normally looked to identify the principles on which successful institutions operate, and then to apply those principles to K-12. Rather, it has taken the institution as it stands even though it lacks entry, lacks choice, lacks incentives for organizations, lacks the 'have to' for change and improvement.

We need now to look further at what are the defining principles of K-12 to see what an unusual and defective system we have for this important institution, and to understand how the structure of 'reasons and opportunities' is out of alignment with the mission the country has given public education to perform.

The 'givens' of the K-12 institution

The principles on which public education was constructed are fairly clear and easy to describe. In recent years many states have begun to change certain of the system principles in fairly significant ways. Policy conflict arises where the new principles collide with the old, challenging the culture developed in the institution over more than a century.

The traditional institution has taken it as given that:

- Constitutionally, education is a responsibility of the state. The state did not, however, create schools. The state made it possible to form districts and the districts then created schools.

- For the students attendance is mandatory, typically from age 7 to age 16 (though in practice most students begin kindergarten at age 5 and most remain in high school until age 18).

- Unlike many of our institutions K-12 education is districted, has boundaries. Kids go to school where they live, though families are free to live where they choose to live (within the limits of what they can afford).

- Within each set of district boundaries there has been a single organization authorized to offer public education. Students enrolled in the schools of that organization. State law gave this organization in effect an 'exclusive franchise' within its territory. K-12 has not been an open institution. It has been set up as essentially a regulated-public-utility arrangement.

- The district organization is a public corporation, owning and operating the schools. Its board is expected both to make policy and to oversee the administration of the schools. The board is a political institution, elected by the people (or in some large cities appointed by an official elected by the people).

- The district organization does not have to earn its revenues from its customers. Public schooling was and is free to the student and family. The district-organization is appropriated its revenues, which are raised mostly from state and local taxpayers.

■ Teachers and other staff are employees of the district organization. It is a boss/worker model. In most states (the South the principal exception) teachers organize and bargain collectively. It is not a professional model: Teachers are not in charge, with the administrators working for them. Professional issues about schooling are treated as management rights reserved to the board, to be implemented by the administrators for whom the teachers work.

■ Both the system and the institution are controlled by the state. District boards appoint their officials and may arrange their administration. But they do not have power to change the functions assigned or the structure in which they operate. For such changes they must return to the Legislature.

These system features, givens for those who work in the K-12 institution, create incentives that interact powerfully with the interests of the organizations and their members to shape the way the institution behaves.

These givens create perverse incentives

The effect of these institutional arrangements and system features, taken together, has been to guarantee the districts and the people in them their customers, their revenues, their jobs, their security; almost everything important to their material success. And this guarantee by the state of the districts' success has been good whether or not they accomplish the mission they have been given to perform. Little really has depended on whether the students learn.[2]

This public-utility arrangement, guaranteeing organizational success, made K-12 an institution that, as Albert Shanker said at the Itasca Seminar in October 1988, "can take its customers for granted". There was not really a 'have to'. And this powerfully shapes the districts' behavior: Organizations that can take their customers and their success for granted can safely put their own interests first.

Where nothing really depended on whether the students learn and where there was, as Shanker said, "nothing at stake" there was little reason for districts to set clear objectives, measure performance and create consequences for performance; to change teacher practices, to introduce new learning technology and to put student interests first.

David K. Cohen of the University of Michigan wrote delicately in 1986 that K-12 contains "weak incentives for the introduction of innovations that would cause internal stress". Proposals for significant change surely do cause internal stress. Change disrupts settled routines. It upsets people. It causes controversy. Controversy produces meetings; keeps people up late at night. It may produce a grievance. It

---

[2]In this and what follows I am essentially summarizing what I wrote in the paper I circulated in 1989: "The States Will Have to Withdraw the Exclusive".

might cause a strike, which could lose an election or damage or even end a career.

Excellence is hard work. Why would we expect organizations to do the hard things that excellence requires—to take risks, upset adults' comfortable routines, challenge powerful interests, put clients first—when nothing makes that necessary? When success is assured an organization becomes inert. It lacks an ability to become what Seymour Sarason has called a "self-correcting" institution.

So as they consider the need for change and proposals for improvement the superintendent, the board, the principal, the union inevitably weigh the potential benefits to the students and to the public against the risk of creating "internal stress". And ask themselves what will happen if they do not change. The risks of change are real. There is not much countervailing that requires students' interests to be put ahead of adult interests; nothing very bad that happens if the decision is to say 'No'. So the incentives are to say 'No'.

Now the new accountability model proposes to introduce a 'have to'; introduces regulations intended to sanction non-performance. This may or may not represent a reason to change. It does violate what has been called the first commandment for those in government: that "Thou shalt not do direct harm"; that a 'have to' can be introduced only indirectly, as a second-order consequence. Harm done directly invites resistance.

Perverse incentives produce bad effects

The decision to work within the traditional givens is a problem. It is not smart for a state to expect performance from an institution in which the rewards are provided whether the mission is accomplished or not. Bad system design causes behaviors that do not well serve either the state or the students or, for that matter, the teachers who work in the schools. It becomes a particularly pressing problem now that policy is insisting for the first time that all children learn, making change and improvement necessary.

Student interests are not put first

Seeing the perverse structure of incentive, that fails to make learning something the organization had to do in its own interest, helps us understand its practices and its behaviors. People who observe these behaviors, and dislike them, sometimes criticize the teachers and the administrators involved. But in fact we are looking at the effect of the faulty system-incentives. These go far to explain both individual and organizational behavior. Specifically:

- Why good teachers and administrators describe the effort to put student interests first as "a risk".
- Why the districts did not themselves set high standards for student and teacher performance.

- Why teacher and school performance was not measured and why compensation is unrelated to performance.

- Why senior teachers get to teach where they want to teach rather than where they may be needed most.

- Why so much of the money for professional development is spent for training driven more by teachers' personal interests than by the needs of the organization.

- Why districts do not intervene decisively to hold a school accountable when students fail to learn.

- Why the 'good things' that are broadly agreed on do not get adopted.

The good people in public education get treated unfairly

This system is unfair both to the public and to the good people who work in the institution. People should never be put in a situation where the incentive-structure is not aligned with the objectives they have been given to accomplish.

A structure of incentives that lets an educational institution put its own interests first exploits teachers' altruism. As Shanker said, "If we work hard and kids do well, nothing particularly good happens. If we don't push we can count on remaining popular with our colleagues". Such a system is unfair to good teachers.

A system that guarantees organizations their success also undercuts leadership. Good superintendents and principals will say to their organizations: "We have to". But the organization knows this is not true: It does not have to. The organization's existence is assured. Why create all the stress?

K-12 is full of good people. Ted Sizer remarks near the end of *Horace's Compromise:* "The people are better than the system". That's true. The people are as good as any. They are working in a bad system. The failure to see this—and to say this—means the people get blamed for the faults of the system. Parents blame teachers and administrators. Educators, in response, blame parents and kids. It is all wrong. We should stop blaming people, stop blaming the schools, stop blaming the institution. We need to fix its system.

The debate can't get to the heart of the problem

Unable internally to face the hard decisions that improvement requires, the institution not surprisingly takes the easy out: It makes money the solution and then blames policymakers when they do not provide 'enough'.[3]

Over the years the argument has been simplified to an assertion educators assume no one will deny: "Money makes a difference". Without more we cannot do

---

[3]Frustrated as chair of the K-12 Finance Committee in Minnesota in the 1990s, Senator Larry Pogemiller asked the districts to say what they would need to get kids to learn. It proved a question the districts did not want to answer.

more; with less we will have to do less. Money is the variable and budget problems should be solved with revenue increases. Inside the box B is a mechanism that turns resources A into results C. But policymakers are steered away from changing the way things are done. The message is: The way we do things cannot change. We are not in the 'different' business, not in the 'productivity' business.

Clearly, though, the mechanism that turns resources into results does affect results. Policymakers can adjust the settings inside the box to make the mechanism work better or less well, more expensively or less expensively. (In a sense this book is about the mechanism inside the box and how to change it.) But it is astonishing how often even intelligent people let themselves be drawn into this "Folks, there are only two choices" fallacy.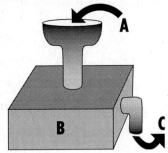

This assertion comes to parents and voters as a proposition to increase the tax levy or the board will cut extracurriculars. It comes to legislatures as the threat that the districts will lay off teachers if the state does not increase their appropriation. In some states layoff notices are often sent out in the critical final weeks of the legislative session. At times the message will be carried to the courts in equity suits ("Our districts are not treated fairly") or in adequacy suits ("Our districts do not get enough").

Over and over the appeal is that the institution cannot do improvement without additional revenue. Existing revenues are committed; we cannot reallocate. To improve we must have more.

The state is endlessly trading money for promises
All this traps policymakers.

Increasing revenue does not necessarily produce improvement. Nor does withholding revenue cause the schools to improve and change. Trying to withhold revenue is a losing game. Appeals to restrain spending are easily countered: Districts simply talk about the importance of education and the needs of the kids; backed up, of course, by political pressures from the teachers.

Governors and legislators like to talk as if they can make districts improve. They can't. They can propose and promise, plead and threaten. They can give money. They can write mandates. But whether the districts respond or not is up to them. Essentially the state has let itself be trapped in a game it cannot win, trading money for promises.

Within the present system and with the traditional strategies for improvement the state gets essentially the appearance of change and improvement. The state accepts the pace at which the district is willing and able to change and improve. And that pace is not very fast.

What we see in all this is not bad people. We see good people acting rationally given the incentives created for them. The state has the incentives in backward. It has failed to align the structure of opportunity and reward with the objectives it has given the institution to perform.

Chapter 3

WHY THE INSTITUTION DEFENDS THE EXISTING SYSTEM

It might seem that the leadership in public education would welcome the state intervening constructively to get the fundamentals right, to create a framework within which boards and administrators would have incentives—reasons and opportunities—to act effectively on the challenges they face.

But this would require those inside to be candid about the problems of the institution. And most are not eager to do that. In public educators are reluctant to talk about the political obstacles to making change—though in private, as someone has noted, they seldom talk about anything else.

Some minds do seem open. But by and large the leadership reacts with hostility if state policy leadership tries to change the arrangements for K-12. And if the state—blocked in its effort to turn this into a self-improving institution—tries to introduce improvements directly into existing schools, the institution resists that intervention as well, waving the banner of local control and complaining that the state is trying to usurp the role of the elected board.

Essentially the attitude is that the state should not intervene in either way: It should give the districts the money and leave them alone.

The state cannot accept that. Pressed now by national legislation it has got to have an institution that works. So the state has to act. But the answer is not to do improvement from the state level. Rather, it is to make K-12 a self-improving institution.

Sources of the defensiveness

In moving to change the incentive structure it will be important for policymakers to understand both the arguments thrown up against an effort to change the givens and the sources from which they spring. What follows may throw some light on the way the institution thinks and on its reasons for trying to dismiss the suggestion that structure and incentives make a difference.

■ They feel criticism of 'the system' is criticism of them

Educators commonly take any comment about 'the system' as a comment about themselves, organizationally and personally. They tend to treat comments as criticism and to treat criticism as hostility. In one meeting the first year of the governor's discussion group[1] in Minnesota the head of the superintendents' association asked others not to talk in terms of change. Someone broke the silence: For heaven's sake why not? "To talk about change", he said, "implies that what went before was not OK."

The problem really is partly language. Too often the tendency of superintendents and others in the institution not to listen well is compounded by the unclarity with which others talk. In one breath a speaker will criticize 'the system' as a monopoly public utility and in the next will use the term 'system' to mean the city schools. Immediately the defenses go up. The analysis or the argument for change is dismissed as a personal attack: not taken seriously, simply not heard. Sometimes the response is to attack the critic: "Not a friend of public education", "a teacher-basher." Many analysts simply saying what is true and important have felt this attack.

This is not a trivial problem. The thinking will not be clear unless the concepts and the language are clear.

■ They find the notion of incentives distasteful

People in public education, especially teachers, think of themselves as altruistic, motivated by the love of teaching and the desire to help students learn. Say 'incentives' and they hear: 'money'. They insist they are not motivated primarily by money. Teachers say they mean well, work hard: Why should they need incentives to do what's right for kids? Board members and administrators, people who see themselves as running the schools, display the same dislike.

In the summer of 1982 Willard Baker asked me to talk to the big summer meeting of the Minnesota School Boards Association (MSBA). He'd just become executive director of MSBA. He'd read some things I'd been writing about public services redesign. That work did not at the time involve K-12. But he was interested in the general idea, and he invited me to give the noon address.

That morning at a meeting of a local foundation working on education I'd heard Larry Pierce talk about that experiment in Florida with site-based decision-making. So I ad-libbed that story into my talk.[2]

---

[1]See pages 109, 140.

[2]See page 17.

Next to me at the head table was Joan Parent: chair of the board in her community for years, former president of MSBA, former president of the National School Boards Association. As I was gathering my papers afterward I was aware of her standing there. She didn't say "Nice talk" or "Thanks-for-coming". She just made reference to that story. "I'd never have handled it like that", she said. "I'd have sent them a directive to turn off the lights and turn off the air conditioning, and if they didn't do it I'd fire them!" And she turned and walked away.

Teachers who believe in altruism and board members who believe in directives have a common dislike of incentives. Perhaps understandably, since the discussion in education does commonly think of incentives as applied to individuals rather than to organizations. This is a problem to which we will return.

■ *Districts have trouble letting their schools 'do different'*

In recent years a recurring proposal has been for districts to give their schools more autonomy, more opportunity to try different and better practices.

As early as the 1970s school principals were pushing for 'school-based decision-making', echoing the conclusion from research that the school should be the unit of improvement. It is an appealing idea. In Britain 'local management of schools' was imposed on the education authorities in 1988. In this country the experience was different.

Allan Odden at the University of Wisconsin finds that when districts give schools personnel the schools do what they had been doing; that when districts give schools dollars the schools do something different, patterns of expenditure change. And, "Patterns of expenditure", says John Myers, the fiscal consultant in Colorado, "are more important than levels of expenditure".

But this idea of autonomy generating improvement runs quite against the common impulse, which is to identify the characteristics of good schools and then tell all schools to do what these good schools do; the impulse to say, as Professor John Goodlad put it in 1994, "Bottle it!" A more sensible response, he observed, would be to identify the conditions that made it possible for those schools to become good schools and then to replicate those conditions.[3] In most cases the key condition seems in fact to have been autonomy: The schools that became good schools either had been given the freedom to make changes themselves or had leaders who simply made decisions at the site.

So the question becomes: How to get autonomy to the school, so that principals and teachers can make changes and improvements quickly—without having to become outlaws operating on the theory that it is easier to ask forgiveness than permission.

---

[3]*Educational Renewal*, Jossey-Bass, 1994, Chapter 7

Here again common sense encounters the prejudice against changing 'structure', encounters the inclination to 'do improvement' rather than to cause improvement by getting the fundamentals right. Late in 2000 a group of leading university educators deplored the initiatives being offered by both candidates for president.[4] Choice (vouchers), reconstitution and new (chartered) schools all miss the point, they said, because they "focus on changing governance and structure rather than on improving teaching and learning". Research shows the way to effective schools, they said: high expectations and standards, curriculum and assessment that fit the standards, strong principals, a safe environment, supportive parents, well-prepared teachers, professional development and "accountability all through the school". There is no guarantee, they said, that structural changes will bring such schools into being. Oh, my.

Within the district the preference for command as a method constrains the real delegation of meaningful authority to the school. Boards and their administrations do not want to relinquish control either of money or of professional issues. So site-management proves more rhetoric than reality. Boards often reset the question as 'shared decision-making'. What results is often a 'site council' through which parents, teachers and other school staff make some decisions about the small proportion of the total school budget that is under real school control.[5]

In Edmonton, Canada, Mike Strembitsky was able to transfer authority to the schools and to put the central service units on an enterprise basis. The Edmonton model was widely known and much admired. But Strembitsky was exceptional; a discontented teacher who went almost directly from the classroom to being superintendent and who stayed there 20 years. Most districts do not have superintendents like that.

Even the little that happens is slow. In 1995 when Sen. Gene Merriam suggested the state intervene to speed along the delegation of authority, all of Minnesota's major education groups appeared in opposition. Not to the idea, of course. "We're not ready", they said. "We need more time, we need more training". Sen. Jerry Janezich looked at the head of the superintendents' association. "Mr. Jensen," he said, "how old will I be when you're ready?"

■ Schools themselves have difficulty 'doing different'

It is not only the central office that resists the effort to make the school the unit of improvement. Not every school wants to be autonomous. Not every principal wants

---

[4]*Christian Science Monitor,* November 7, 2000.

[5]Beginning in fall 2004 it will be possible for Minnesotans to compare on the state department's website the revenue in each school—arriving with the students who enroll there—and the amount spent in each school, reflecting actual rather than average teacher salaries. This will spotlight the effect of district budgeting and personnel policies, on schools and students.

to take risks. Not everyone is comfortable with the implied requirement to perform and to be accountable, on which continued autonomy will depend. And not all teachers are comfortable making major changes in the classroom.

The culture of traditional practice that makes it hard for the district to change the schools makes it hard also for the school to change itself.

The design of traditional school is shaped, Richard Elmore of the Harvard Graduate School of Education writes powerfully, by the basic conceptions of teaching and learning, by "the core of educational practice: how teachers understand the nature of knowledge and the student's role in learning, how these ideas about knowledge and learning are manifested in teaching and classwork".

> "Teachers tend to think of knowledge as discrete bits of information about a particular subject and of student learning as the acquisition of this information through processes of repetition, memorization and regular testing of recall. . . The teacher, who is generally the center of attention in the classroom, initiates most of the talk and orchestrates most of the interaction in the classroom around brief factual questions, if there is any discussion at all. . . Often students are grouped by age, and again within age groups according to their perceived capabilities to acquire information. The latter is generally accomplished either by within-class ability groups or, at higher grade levels, in 'tracks' or clusters of courses comprised of students whom teachers judge to have similar abilities. . . Individual teachers are typically responsible for one group of students for a fixed period. Seldom working in groups to decide what a given group of students should know or how that knowledge should be taught, teachers are typically solo practitioners operating in a structure that feeds them students and expectations about what students should be taught. Students' work is typically assessed by asking them to repeat information that has been conveyed to them by the teacher in the classroom, usually in the form of worksheets or tests that involve discrete, factual, right-or-wrong answers.[6]

The inadequacies in current practice lead some to advocate a large program of professional development, to get teachers to do what research tells us works, so children will learn basic skills. But it may simply not be possible to organize and manage so large and complex a program for the nation's more than two million teachers.

Long-established conceptions about schooling do not change easily. And it is not only teachers who are reluctant to change. There are people who do not want teachers trying new things, and lots of people outside who want school to remain the way they remember it. Existing practice is the kind of school in which most of us

---

[6]"Getting to Scale with Successful Educational Practices", Chapter 9 in *Rewards and Reform*, Susan Fuhrman and Jennifer O'Day, editors; Jossey-Bass, San Francisco 1996.

involved in the current discussion grew up, and in which most of us did well. Most of our friends did. We know the people who run the schools. We like them. We support them. We are not much inclined to push them to change what worked for us. The result, as Joe Graba says, is that while almost everybody wants the schools to be better almost nobody wants them to be different. Not appearing too different thus becomes essential for the district, to maintain the legitimacy necessary for its political success.[7]

■ There's a belief 'school' doesn't need to be different

The tendency is to insist that public education is a successful institution. Criticism, even implied, is resented particularly by people in higher-income suburban districts. In talking about the schools you are expected to separate these districts from whatever problem there may be elsewhere. Privately those inside the districts sometimes tell a different story. But publicly the correct line is: Most schools are OK.

People are more willing to acknowledge problems in the cities. But quickly the argument is that these do not mean a problem with the schools; rather, that problems are created by the new and different students coming to the schools. There is a lot of talk—rather more nicely put—about rotten kids, rotten parents and rotten society. Board members talk in code about how 'mobile' the new families are. Superintendents talk about the number of different languages spoken in different students' homes—almost always as a problem. With the kids they've had for a while, district officials say, the schools are doing fine. It is a bit like the old conviction in the auto industry that accidents were caused by careless drivers—before the 1960s when it became clear that some responsibility for accidents had to be accepted also by those who design the cars and by those who design the roads.

This conviction melds with another deeply held conviction, which you often find in the teachers and administrators you most like and most respect. It is that school is not responsible for what the students learn. Kids are in school a small fraction of the time between age 5 and age 18, the argument runs. Many things shape their learning, school but one of them. Whether students learn and want to learn is up to them, is beyond our control. They resist the assumption that teachers are to be held accountable for student learning rather than for best professional practice. This is another important question to which we will return.

To the extent that school is not all right it is, educators are quick to say, because the state has failed to provide the support they need. So to troubled families and kids add stingy legislators and taxpayers. They're the problem. Again: School is OK.

---

[7]See page 37.

People in business may recognize this as the eternal complaint of managers in a failing division: We're all right. Our problem is those demanding customers, unreliable suppliers and difficult employees. What we need is a central office that understands our problems and gives us loyal support and additional resources.

■ *Education could not change its system, even should it wish*

Even if education wanted to change its system it couldn't. Cities can and since the 1970s counties can, through the 'charter commission' process or sometimes by action of their governing bodies. Not districts. There is no concept of home rule in public education.

A board of education can change its administration—the district's internal organization. But neither the boards nor the people of the community can reach the legal structure of the institution or the incentive-structure of the system. The changes they can make, do make, are a kind of tinkering-within-the-givens.

This inability to make significant change either in the organization or in the institution of course reinforces the disposition of the leadership anyway to take present arrangements as given: Why spend time talking about what cannot happen? This may also be what causes some influential professors of education to say that structure, governance, does not make a difference. All they see is the tinkering, and they observe correctly that this has no significant effects. Like the K-12 leadership they assume traditional arrangements and do not contemplate the givens being changed in more than incremental ways.

Change-oriented superintendents, board members, principals and teachers might, of course, go to the legislature to try to secure the changes that are needed. But they really have neither the time nor the inclination to do that. On matters involving only their particular district, yes: Going to the Legislature to get a local bill is well accepted. But a single district going to the Legislature to press for a change in the general law affecting K-12 would be quite a different matter. It is the associations that are expected to speak on questions about the institution. The associations are not keen on individual members showing up at the state Capitol to speak their own minds.

Educators as individuals might try to affect the positions of their associations. But this is also unlikely.[8] Board members trying to persuade the association to restructure public education would be undertaking a third job, after their district responsibilities and their personal careers. Superintendents would be undertaking a second job, after their responsibilities to their districts. There is sometimes the impulse. I remember a long lunch in the '80s with Dale Hauch, then superintend-

---

[8]See Chapter 12.

ent in the North St. Paul/Maplewood district. It was during a legislative session. He saw the importance of the system issues we were discussing. But it was simply too much. At the end he said, sadly: "I have no time to think about these questions".

Many are not even moved to try. They find their own interests deeply vested in the existing arrangements: their incomes, their retirement, their job security, their careers, their reputations, their professional relationships. To go against all this, to go against their colleagues and their own associations, would be an extraordinary act of leadership.

So system change is nobody's first job. Worse, the other institutions expected to provide leadership are disappearing. The university is no longer looked to as a leader on K-12 public education: not its president and perhaps not even its dean of education. Many university lab schools have been closed. State commissioners of education today are less often superintendents or even educators, governors having taken away from state boards of education the power to appoint. In Minnesota the state board of education is gone.

■ *They feel they can hold off outside pressure for change*
The remaining possibility has been that major change might be imposed on K-12 through legislation generated by others from the outside.

Historically the institution has had reason to feel confident about its ability to defeat such efforts. Public education—at least after the reforms of the Progressive Era—was substantially removed from the normal processes of politics. Where boards were elected the races were often at-large, with citizen committees to advise voters about 'good candidates'. In some cities boards were appointed; in Pittsburgh by the Court of Common Pleas. In Kansas City, after the scandals of 1910-11 board members were agreed on jointly by—of all things—the county committees of the political parties, in an arrangement in which the dominant Pendergast organization guaranteed the schools an independence from the normal political pressure for jobs, contracts and campaign contributions.[9] The popularity of the institution was reinforced after World War II as children of the baby boom flooded into new schools. More people were finishing high school. Budgets grew as education exerted a primary claim on public resources. All this drew on a deep reservoir of support for public education. Business, the foundations, the civic leadership, the media of communications all displayed an unshakable loyalty.

Over time the institution grew skilled at reinforcing this. Year after year while he was executive director of the National School Boards Association Tom Shannon's

---

[9]Homer Wadsworth, by then head of the Cleveland Foundation, recalled this arrangement in 1991 from his 14 years on the board in Kansas City.

response to critics was to explain that public education, the school board, is the foundation of American democracy. Who would tamper with the foundation of American democracy?

The risk of standing pat was fairly low. The influentials in the community were seldom uncomfortable: Their kids were doing well and if they had a personal problem they could usually get the school or the teacher-assignments they wanted. Key groups at both the local and the national level were fairly easily co-opted. Little pressure was felt from consumers and their advocates.

For years this worked; gave public education a capacity to protect itself that few other institutions enjoyed. Businesses have to worry about the appearance of new competitors, and are constrained both legally and politically from trying too aggressively to protect their own preferred position. The K-12 system is set in law and can be changed only through a political process that until recently those in the institution were fairly confident they could control.

In the 1960s and '70s a few doubting books appeared: *Why Johnny Can't Read* and *Up the Down Staircase* were bestsellers. In the '70s, as the influence of old elites waned, new pressures for 'participation' created pressure for district representation. But in the '70s the spread of teacher-unionization reinforced the institution at key points where change might be introduced: in the elections for members of the district board and for members of the state legislatures. So public discontent might grow and yet still not significantly threaten the institution's defenses against change.

So long as education retained this special status the assignment for the superintendent was fairly simple: Talk about your vision, always be trying somewhere every new thing being written-up favorably, keep the board together, keep the tax rate under control, avoid scandals. Stay tight with traditional notions. Teach kids what adults think kids should know. All this was helped by the fact that in those days families were more inclined to accept what they were given, and by the fact that—though there was lots of testing—little was really known about student performance. James Lytle, then in the central office in Philadelphia summed it up in 1992: To give its alienated students the kind of school in which they would succeed would make the big-city district look not-legitimate in the eyes of those on whom it depends for its financial and political support. Caught between the needs of its students and its own need for legitimacy it elects to look legitimate.[10]

In 1986 Dan Loritz got me together for breakfast with a teachers union leader. We talked that Saturday morning about the system problems and the need for

---

[10]See "Prospects for Reforming Urban Schools", Urban Education, July 1992.

change; talked, as I remember, until about 11 a.m. At end, the man looked at us, sighed and said: "Of course, we do have the option to stonewall it."

And until recently they did.

■ *Most cannot conceive of a fundamentally different system*

Part of the reason that individuals in the K-12 institution defend the existing system is that it is very hard for them to imagine any other. Districting, the exclusive franchise, the board the owner-operator of all the schools, teachers employees, school as courses and classes . . . all this has been the framework of life for as long as those in the institution can remember.

Many of those who work in education have little experience working in other sectors of community life. Some have spent all their careers in this institution, sometimes in one district. Their background and experience can be quite narrow: as a student, then in training, then teaching, then perhaps a principal or district administrator. Lateral recruitment in K-12, the recent trend toward bringing in superintendents from other fields, is exceptional—as the term used to describe it suggests: These are 'non-traditional' superintendents.

Background shapes the way people think. In the late 1980s Gov. Perpich created a task force to consider the personnel implications of a further consolidation of districts in rural Minnesota. It was a mixed group: educators and business people. At one point a superintendent said that in responding to the enrollment decline in his own district he had concluded the only practical course was to follow seniority absolutely. Anything else would destroy morale in the organization, he said. An executive at General Mills responded that just the reverse would be true in his organization. What would destroy morale during a reduction in staff would be to go by seniority "since everybody knows who the good producers are". The two then looked across the gulf between them.

At one point I was asked to talk about school-based-management to a regional meeting of superintendents in Minnesota. It did not seem a good idea to go into that meeting alone, so I asked Ron Hubbs to come along. He had just retired from the St. Paul Companies, where as CEO he had been known for decentralizing and delegating authority. He started by telling the superintendents how his mother and his grandmother had been public school teachers. He then explained how much better an organization works if you delegate both authority and responsibility. Decisions are better informed and more rapid. It avoids bureaucracy "which afflicts business too". It frees up the central office for bigger questions. It makes the sites more of a team: "We will not let a person dissatisfied with a local manager's decision jump to the home office." The superintendents were less than enthusiastic. "If we let other people make the decisions", one of them asked Hubbs, "some of those decisions will be wrong, and how can we permit that?"

The difficulty in thinking in unconventional terms is a problem in discussions not only about the district but also about the school. People struggle to imagine computers doing what teachers do: 'delivering instruction'. The assumption that "We must achieve computer use in an institutional arrangement that has many difficulties in making such large transformations" produces questions like, "How is the problem of introducing computers resolved within the professional, sociocultural, bureaucratic environment that exists?".[11] The idea of changing the institutional arrangement—say, of creating a different kind of school compatible with the new electronics—is outside the box, is not traditional thinking.

In fairness, it is not only educators who have difficulty with new approaches. Old conceptions block off new ideas in many fields.

I remember listening once to a doctor from Kansas City describe the new model of medical education introduced with the creation of the medical school at the University of Missouri there: Admit students right out of high school, let them see patients their first day and graduate them in six years with a bachelor's degree and as safe doctors. A terrible idea, the chief of surgery of Hennepin County General Hospital immediately told him. The doctor from Kansas City looked at the chief of surgery for a time and then, exactly as if pronouncing a medical diagnosis, said: "You have a locked mind".

Aeronautical engineers were defeated by the idea of human-powered flight, for which Henry Kremer, a British industrialist was offering prizes in the 1970s. Paul MacCready won the big prize in 1979 when a man pedaled his Gossamer Albatross 22 miles across the English Channel. When asked why he succeeded where others failed, MacCready concluded that the engineers' training got in their way. They were taught to make aircraft safe. This of course made them heavy. Lacking a training in structures, MacCready could see that safety was not a concern for an aircraft carrying one man 10 feet in the air at 10 miles an hour. He concluded people are hemmed in by their preconceptions. "There is very little in our schools and our culture that forces us to get away from established patterns and look at things in different ways . . . We need to be skeptical and try different routes to solve problems." [12]

Can this resistance survive?

Resisting a rethinking was a practical policy for the organizations in K-12 so long as students had to come, so long as revenues rose steadily, so long as nothing happened

---

[11]"Facing the Hard Facts", Educational Testing Service, 2002.
[12]"Putting the Wings on Man", *Yale Alumni Magazine*, 1980.

if students really didn't learn, so long as nobody really knew whether the students were learning or not, so long as schools could count on well-behaved students from solid families, so long as districts had the exclusive franchise for public education.

Resistance serves the institution less well today, given the changes now putting pressure on it. The students are different now. Collective bargaining has appeared. Desegregation happened. There is tougher competition for revenues. Enrollment is turning down again. Parent choice is becoming a reality. The Internet and the web let young people access learning directly. Now the accountability model has arrived: standards, testing and consequences. We will look at these changes in Chapter 4.

The institution still does not want to acknowledge a problem with present system arrangements, and still resists when the state attempts to change those arrangements. Because others, outside, are raising doubts about the institution many insiders feel that, as a loyal parent campaigning for a tax increase in a big suburban district in Minnesota put it, "We have to create certainty."

But continued resistance by the institution probably could not stop the changes being made by societal forces and by public policy. Resistance would mean only that the needed new arrangements would have to be—in the nice distinction the English make—imposed on the institution rather than agreed with the institution.

So a key question today is whether the old resistance will remain, trying still to hold the institution in its present arrangements, or whether new attitudes will appear, interested in enlarging K-12's capacity to adapt.

Clearly major changes can be imposed. Collective bargaining was imposed. So was desegregation. It will be harder that way; it would be easier if the institution would agree that adaptation is essential to its survival. But the change can be imposed.

The pressures are building on state leadership to do that and the states are beginning to move.

■ ■ ■ ■ ■ ■

Chapter **4**

NOW THE OLD SYSTEM FEELS NEW PRESSURES FOR CHANGE

Within the districts the impulse is still to try to draw on the reservoir of support for the old arrangements that served the country so well for so long. But as time goes on the effectiveness of the traditional defense is declining.

The conventional effort to improve school has been tried and found wanting: the effort to 'do' improvement directly by adding into the K-12 institution as traditionally structured better training, more research, more demonstrations, better dissemination, higher standards, measurement of performance, different curriculum, better technology.

All these good things are needed, of course. What is troubling is how many of these good-things the institution did not do itself; how many were done only after appeals for outside help, and how many had to be pushed at the districts from the outside.

The institution continues to find explanations for the slow pace of improvement. But difficulties cannot be an excuse for not changing. The effort to lay off the blame onto the students or onto outside forces is no longer acceptable. People understand that the schools do now face a more difficult challenge. But they also think school makes a difference and that improving school has to be a part of the solution. Policy can reach, can do more about, school than it can do about television, family structure, the youth culture and the economy.

Most organizations in most institutions do the good things that need to be done: invest in research, seek out best practice, set standards, inspect results, reward good performance, sanction poor performance, train new leadership, cope with the challenge of change. If public education doesn't, why doesn't it?

In this situation trying yet again to do for public education the things it seems unable to do for itself really is the equivalent of doing your daughter's homework: a misdirected kindness, clearly the wrong way to help. Slowly it is becoming obvious that the basic system-arrangement is responsible for the organizations not making the improvements they need to be making, not adapting to the new situation that now challenges them. Logic says: Find what is responsible for this failure, and fix that.

The state has switched its signals

For years public education had successfully resisted measurement. Kids took tests, of course, lots of them. The deal was: different tests everywhere. Or if the same test was given in several districts: no public reporting of the results. One way or another, no comparisons. When Jack Merwin came to the University of Minnesota after heading the National Assessment of Educational Progress he was candid about the intense resistance to comparisons even at the broadest level, across states.

Measurement was bound to come in, of course, once the requirement for improved student performance came in. There was some thought that testing could be held off until the standards were in place, on the argument that measurement should begin only after the country had agreed on what students should know. Standards are controversial and consensus takes time, so perhaps a debate over standards might hold off the introduction of measurement.

If this was indeed the hope it was disappointed. Baseline testing, to measure how students were performing before the standards came in, was introduced in many states; in Minnesota in 1996. It is this testing—a single test, given statewide, with results compared and published—that has shown so clearly the surprisingly low levels of student proficiency.

With the introduction of the accountability model the state was switching its signals. The old understanding between the state and the districts was that the state would not really keep score. Kids would have to come to school and districts would have to offer a basic set of courses. But the state would not insist on student performance. Now, suddenly, the givens had changed, and there were new questions being asked and having to be answered.

Testing has exposed low performance

What the new testing shows about the levels of student performance has made a big impression on the public.

Inner-city communities now see how poorly their children have been doing, even though per-pupil spending is often high. This has outraged and activated some advocates for the low-income and minority community. Listen to Gary Sudduth, then president of the Minneapolis Urban League, speaking to the Minneapolis board of education in the spring of 1997:

> "For the second year in a row two-thirds of the eighth-grade students failed the Basic Skills Tests. Most of those students were African-American children. . . Eighteen of

the 21 schools that include eighth grade could not pass the test. At Folwell 85% failed. At Richard Green, 70%; the same for Northeast. Even at one of our leading magnet schools, Sheridan Elementary, over 73% of the students failed math and over 65% failed reading. . . It doesn't really matter whether [the superintendent] is here tonight, or next month, or next year. You are responsible for the Minneapolis school district. You made the campaign promises. You are responsible for where the money goes. You are responsible for setting policy. You are responsible for the results of those policies. You members of the school board, each of you, had as your primary campaign promise that the gap in test scores would be closed. You have committed to ensure that all kids learn."

The board's response was to change the superintendent and to promise to do better.

The impact of the test results was not confined to the central cities. In all kinds of Lake Wobegon communities in Minnesota a third or more of the kids could not pass the Basic Skills Tests in reading and math. These were not particularly difficult tests. Perhaps for this reason there was little objection when the state made them a requirement for graduation; fairly casually, not thinking this would really be a problem. But as kids continued to fail in significant numbers at 9th grade, at 10th grade, at 11th grade, anxiety mounted. Legislators did not need to be persuaded it would be very serious politically if they had to tell 20 per cent or 15 per cent or even 10 per cent of the parents that their daughter or son was not going to get a diploma.

With heroic efforts, especially with summer school, most of the students were gotten up to 'passing' on the 8th grade test in time to get their diploma. It is a hollow victory: If students are barely at 8th grade level as they finish 12th grade, how much have they gotten, really, out of high school?

The public's expectations have risen

As more and more test-results made the headlines a common response from defenders of the institution has been to insist that the schools have in fact been doing better than in the past. They insisted that the criticism—or the implication—that student performance had fallen, that schools are not as good as they once were, is simply untrue. Those carrying this message became popular speakers at meetings where educators gather.

But when the superintendent from Baton Rouge made an impassioned statement to this effect at a meeting in New Orleans late in the '80s, he was brought up short by Phil Schlechty, director of the Center for Leadership and School Reform in Louisville, Ky., Schools are better, Schlechty said, but not as good as the country needs them to be.

Joe Graba, then dean of the graduate school of education at Hamline University in Saint Paul, explained the dissatisfaction this way, to the Minnesota Rural Education Association in 1998:

"Some time in the late 1970s knowledge became the major strategic resource, as land was in the agricultural era. This fact has attracted the attention of the political and business leadership to the quality of our learning enterprise. They are dissatisfied with what they see.

"Our response was to say that they were wrong. We pointed out how much better we are than we were in the 1950s. We were right about that. But this linear comparison, which we like to make, is not persuasive with a customer. The customer is not interested in whether we are better now than in the past. The customer is interested in whether we are as good as he needs us to be. And in truth the needs of the society have been increasing faster than education has been improving."

Tom Nelson, former superintendent at Buffalo, Minn., and before that the state commissioner of education, remembers an executive at Northwestern Bell Telephone Company saying that in the years when the company was a monopoly its surveys always showed customer satisfaction high. Then came deregulation. Both products and service changed and improved. But in surveys the customers now said they were less satisfied and wanted improvement.

"Running faster, only to fall further behind", says Paul Houston, executive director of the American Association of School Administrators.

'Money' no longer seems a magic bullet

The simple assertion that money makes the difference can be especially unpersuasive for the parents of poor children in the cities. Money has been increased, steadily, in real terms, over recent decades.

Listen again to Gary Sudduth:

"I am outraged because once again we have been betrayed by the very institution that holds out the promise of a better future for our children." (He then detailed the promises made.) "I'm here tonight to tell you time has run out . . .

"In the past six years the Minneapolis district has spent, in addition to its regular budget, over $228 million in compensatory funds, $174 million from the referendum, $66 million in Title I funds, $114 million in desegregation funds, and that doesn't include special education money. All that money, we were told, would be allocated to close the gap, level the playing field, all the other cliches. That's over $500 million in the last six years. Where did all that money go? Show me the connection between all that money and so little learning. Surely if all those millions went to the students who showed poorer performance there would be no gap. Show me the money! Where did it go?"[1]

Journalists and other advocates often point to the inadequate buildings and the ill-prepared teachers and the obsolete books and materials in low-wealth districts. And reasonable people agree this would seem to justify higher spending. The question is: Where would the added revenue actually get spent? This returns us to the central fact that the K-12 institution is not built to put student learning first. Realists understand: There are other uses for the money. A board of education faces demands from its customers and demands from its employees. Too often this trade-off is not made in the interest of the students. In Minnesota everyone understands the boards are not going to take a strike. They have decided they cannot win a strike, so they see no point in making demands or in resisting demands where to do so might cause a strike.

The Minnesota Association of School Administrators said with simple candor in 1991: Districts are "unable to contain (their) costs". Biennial salary settlements exceed new revenue; program and staff are adjusted to bring expenses into line. Superintendents then go to the Legislature for more money, in which effort the political support of the teachers union is essential. Periodically the superintendents talk about trying to change the bargaining law in ways that would constrain expenditure. But the decision is always the same: "We need the teachers this year. Why piss 'em off?" Nothing changes. Next bargaining round it happens all over again, as boards appeal for 'adequate' financing. No wonder legislators ask themselves: What is the concept of filling a bucket that has a hole in the bottom?

Most people in most organizations in most institutions live with the reality of limited resources; cannot simply ask for additional revenue; have to contain their costs. They are bound to have a limited patience for education's inability to explain—to Gary Sudduth or to others—the connection between more money and better learning. And for its traditional cry that if it does not have more it must do less; that it cannot reallocate, that the way of doing things cannot change.

Can't blame 'problems beyond our control'
Sympathy is bound to be limited, too, for explanations that simply blame the kids.

It's not that kids today aren't a challenge: Of course they are. Especially in the cities there are more kids from different races (which partly means, races different than the teachers') and more different nations. American teenagers have grown up with television, automobiles, drugs, the sexual revolution and what Daniel

---

[1]Tragically, Gary Sudduth died a few weeks later. No voice since has been really angry.

Yankelovich called "the ethic of self-fulfillment".[2] Our schools used to be filled with children, says Mary Lee Fitzgerald, former commissioner in New Jersey. Now, she told the EdVentures meeting in Madison, Wis., in 1999, high schools are filled with young people who are really adults, being treated still as children.

Adjusting to these changes is very difficult for schools. But so is it for every institution. Schools are not the only establishments affected by this change in their customers. Wal-Mart and Target stores are, grocery retailers are, McDonalds and other restaurants are, hotels are, employers are, the Army, Navy, Air Force and Marines are, coaches are, the police are, the kids' neighbors are, where they live. For all of these, the behavior of young people is a reality: Like it or not these institutions know they have to adjust. People in these other institutions can reasonably ask why the schools should not adjust as well.

The change in the character of its customers is not an acceptable excuse for failing to change the K-12 institution: The institution has to adapt—or be adapted, by the states that determine its structure and its system arrangements.

It is fair to hold school accountable

The day Dean Robert Bruininks presented the accountability design that the University of Minnesota College of Education had developed for the state, a teacher reminded him that teachers cannot make students learn. She asked him the predictable question: "How can we be held accountable for things we do not control?"

This is the traditional argument against making the institution responsible for student performance. It is an important question. There is a reasonable answer.

What the teachers say is true, about school being only a part of a student's life: 11 percent of it, some calculate, between ages five and 18. Still, school makes a difference. It is within the ability of a school to improve the teaching it provides, and teachers can influence the student's desire to learn. The school can be judged for what it does and does not do. And the district that owns the schools can be judged for what its schools do and fail to do. The failure to learn cannot be laid off entirely onto 'factors beyond our control'.

Think about baseball.

Imagine a fielder coming back to the dugout after booting his third straight chance and saying to the manager, "The batters are hitting the ball too hard. They don't hit it where I am. Sometimes the ball bounces funny. Last time the sun got in

---

[2]See *New Rules: Searching for Self-fullfillment in a World Turned Upside Down*; Random House, New York 1981.

my eyes." The manager is going to tell him: I expect you to field your position. Nobody fields 1.000: Errors happen. But there is a big difference between fielding .985 and fielding .925. In baseball you are accountable for that difference. Make too many errors, too many more than other players, and there will be consequences. And not unfairly.

The key here is percentages or, put another way, the difference between goals and standards. In baseball the goal is to get a hit every time at bat and to field cleanly every ball hit to you. But nobody realistically expects that goal to be reached even at the major-league level. The practical question becomes: What rate of success is OK? Baseball has a standard, a sense of what average is OK.

The fact that the school cannot make students learn—that poor parenting and bad health and multiple languages and student mobility present serious obstacles to learning—does not relieve the school of its responsibility. Most of us are expected, and expect ourselves, to succeed in the face of obstacles. Nobody will succeed every time. But we're expected to succeed, expect ourselves to succeed, a reasonable proportion of the time. The key is probabilities, percentages and progress toward the goal.

The education discussion should be clearer about the distinction between goals and standards. The goal is for every child to learn. The standard set for school performance can be different, can be more realistic about how many will learn and how well. No school, no teacher, is going to succeed with every student. And the standards can vary for different schools and for different students. There can be appropriate adjustments for the different levels of preparation with which kids enter school, an additional weighting for degree of difficulty as in a diving competition. Or the measure can be rate of gain—value added—rather than the absolute level of performance.

After all the allowances are made, however, there does remain a concept of organizational performance and of organizational failure. Schools can do things to get kids to want to learn, can adjust the way they do things to stimulate the students' interest. Schools must try. Schools make a difference. Districts can fairly be held accountable for their schools: for the autonomy they provide and for the resources they allocate to them.

Students now have other ways to learn

Until the '90s improvement pretty much meant what it had always meant: better teachers, smaller classes, perhaps modest changes in the curriculum: New Math or whatever. There was always some talk about equipment, but after films and film-strips and television and VCRs in the classroom turned out not to revolutionize learning, technology was not a priority on the improvement agenda. Even computers played a relatively minor role until the arrival of the Internet and the World Wide Web.

Then suddenly in the mid-1990s the computer was not any longer simply something to learn how to program or a textbook on a disk. It became the portal through which a student had access to enormous resources of information. As late as about 1995 there were only about 30,000 websites; by 2002 there were something like 30 million.

The implications are profound, both exhilarating and threatening to those who run schools. Students can now be directly in contact with a world of material. School libraries cannot begin to rival what is available on the web. Textbooks and teachers can be disintermediated. Students can be put directly in contact with material, at school or at home; any time of day. Lots of students know how computers work, perhaps better than teachers.

In May 1991 Albert Shanker anticipated this at the gathering to mark the first anniversary of Saint Paul's new Saturn School.

Other countries succeed by tracking kids, he said. But we're (rightly) unwilling to do what Germany does. So from fifth grade on the American teacher has to work with classes containing a wide range of abilities. It is impossible to teach that kind of group by talking. If the teacher talks to the average-and-below s/he loses the bright kids. If s/he talks to the bright kids s/he loses the others. Unfortunately this is what most teachers do: talk.

Learning has to be individualized, he said. "The one-room school was a better learning institution than the classroom we have today". Kids worked at their own pace. The teacher coached. Kids helped each other. But we will not go back to one-room schools. And we cannot hire a teacher for every six kids. Technology is the way out, he said. To avoid tracking, to get away from teacher-talk and to individualize; to let kids work together.

The sudden arrival of the World Wide Web makes Shanker's vision realizable; destroys the old argument that schooling need not and cannot significantly change. It calls into question the notion that students learn mainly from teachers, and that schooling must be group work. It powerfully challenges the institution to find a way now to realize the potential of the new opportunity to put students directly in touch with information and so to individualize learning.[3]

The web is available in school. Students can use it on their own and schools can use it to buy online courses for their students. It is available also to young people

---

[3]After seeing some writer complain that kids cannot learn about Islam because their teachers have not themselves been taught about Islam I went on Google and typed in 'Islam'. In .07 seconds it gave me "about 1,760,000" entries.

outside school, at home and elsewhere. Minnesota now has a tax-credit program that pays for study outside school; even for computer hardware and software.

As choice appears the politics change

The most contentious issue about changing the system has concerned the principle of choice: which parents may select the schools their children attend and which schools these may be. In this area opinion has been shifting quite sharply.

The experience in Minnesota was a tip-off. Even when Gov. Rudy Perpich in 1985 proposed not vouchers but public-sector open enrollment among districts, he was clearly going against opinion as recorded in the polls. Quickly after inter-district open enrollment went into operation, however, public opinion swung sharply behind the Perpich plan. Choice virtually disappeared as a controversial issue. Partly, education groups saw its popularity. Partly they recognized that too many people now understood where the high ground is on the equity effects of choice.[4]

The same thing has been happening nationally.

■ The change in the findings of the Gallup organization's surveys for *The Kappan* magazine reflects this shift in public opinion. Into the mid-1980s they still showed less than majority support for vouchers, for the government paying for students in private schools. Then in 1989, after Gov. Perpich had brought the idea of choice into public education, Gallup asked a different question: "Would you like to be able to choose the public school your children attend?" The response came back 2:1 in favor. The individual in charge of polling for the Associated Press objected that this asked people if they would like to have a right and that people will always say 'Yes' when offered a right. So the question was changed to read, "Do you think people should be able to choose the public school their children attend in your community regardless of where they live?" Arguably this loaded the question. *(The Kappan* is not particularly supportive of choice.) But support remained at 2:1 'Yes'.

■ In 1998 and 1999 after Wisconsin, Ohio and Florida had enacted laws permitting certain students in certain schools to enroll in non-public schools at public expense, *The Kappan* went back to testing support for vouchers. In 1999 it found support had risen, most notably among African-Americans. Lowell Rose, long the executive of Phi Delta Kappa, was fascinated to find that choice was not so much a conservative idea appealing to Republicans as it was an idea appealing to the Democratic constituency. And quite rationally: Well-to-do people can choose suburbs.

This rise in public support for choice in the cities could affect the politics of education. The breakouts in the 1989 Gallup poll showed the groups in the popu-

---

[4]See page 145.

lation in which support for public-school choice rose above 2:1: big cities, rural/farm occupations, public-school parents, people who themselves have not been educated beyond high school, people of median and below-median income and people in communities of color. And the 'Yes' response was perfectly inversely proportional by age: The younger the respondents the stronger the support for being able to choose the school their children attend.

Everyone understands: This is the Democratic constituency. The problem of low student performance, the kids most at risk in the schools, the parental dissatisfaction, the strongest support for change and for choice; all are in the heart of that Democratic constituency. The struggle to respond is fascinating to watch.

Will Marshall, the president of the Progressive Policy Institute, saw the implications and spotted the potential of the idea of public-school choice for Democrats early in the work he and the Democratic Leadership Council were doing to get Bill Clinton elected in 1992. It was proposed in their policy book, *Mandate for Change*. Marshall's efforts had much to do with Clinton's support of chartering as a form of public school choice.

In the fall of 1998 the U.S. Department of Education tested with its civil rights constituency its proposed support for public-school choice and chartering in the reauthorization of the Elementary and Secondary Education Act. There was no basic opposition. The reality (if not quite the desirability) of choice was accepted: "It is now a market out there. We have got to increase the supply of quality public schools", said Bella Rosenberg of the American Federation of Teachers.

But the community most affected is also divided. In big cities much of the leadership and of the teaching force is now African-American. This can suppress, among blacks and whites alike, an impulse to be critical. It did not deter the reform effort in Chicago in 1988. And some individual elected officials have clearly moved: In 1996 on the last night of the legislative session Rep. Dwight Evans brought the Philadelphia black delegation over for Gov. Tom Ridge's charter-schools bill. But the debate is complex and intense.

Is all this enough to cause improvement?
All these forces present new reasons to change. They reinforce what state policy leadership is doing to introduce a new incentive-structure and what the national government is doing now with its hammer of accountability.

Yet these forces by themselves will not produce the improvements we want. Having a reason is not enough. The institution must also have the capacity to change. The challenge now for policy is to provide that capacity, transforming K-12 into a self-improving institution.

PART TWO

HOW TO CREATE
A SELF-IMPROVING
INSTITUTION

Chapter 5

CHANGE 'SCHOOL' SO IT WILL MOTIVATE STUDENTS

To increase the capacity of the institution to change and to increase the capacity of students to learn we will need to do some serious re-thinking about the nature of schooling.

The current discussion is filled with old concepts about what a good school is and ought to be. Think about the way school is so often pictured in articles about improvement: the classroom with desks in rows, the teacher facing the students, talking.

Some people will always want this model. But this conventional notion of school, of instruction in the sense of teachers 'delivering' education (in the old phrase, "filling the child's empty head with learning") is not the only right notion of school. Certainly it is not the only way young people learn.[1]

Improvements on this traditional model may not work for the kids that up to now have been quitting school (or not learning even though they remain enrolled) and for those who could move faster and learn more than they now do. For both, something else needs to be tried. We can't be sure at the start what that is. The answer, as usual in situations of uncertainty, is to try a lot of different things.

Let's begin with the general case for different kinds of schooling and then go on to the question of how to make it possible for different models to appear in schools.

Different kids need different schools

States now say all kids will learn; federal law promises there will be "no child left behind". This asks school to succeed with young people who are different than most of those it worked with successfully in the past. In the past the students who did not relate well to traditional school left. Some went into alternative programs. Mostly

---

[1]School doesn't, can't, 'deliver education' to young people. Like parents, school influences young people. Farmers don't really grow corn, Dan Loritz likes to say; they help corn grow.

they quit. (Kids talk about 'quitting' school, as they talk about 'ditching' school for the rest of the day. 'Dropping out' is an adult term.) Good work was available in those days. Today good work is less available. If we now seriously intend for these young people to stay, and graduate, and achieve at high levels, something will have to change. Will it be the student? Or will it be the school?

Traditional educators have not thought mainly about adapting school to students. The more common idea has been that students should adapt to school, or that somehow the community should send the schools better kids. District officials encourage pre-school 'readiness' programs (separately financed), talk about the community improving housing and social services and stress the importance of better parenting and of 'reducing mobility'.

But the districts will continue to get students who will be a challenge for the traditional model. If you want a sense of kids in school these days read Elinor Burkett's *Another Planet*, bearing in mind as you do that the author is describing a middle-class suburban high school, not an inner-city school. It will quickly correct any notion that even with standards teenagers in conventional school are likely to focus mainly on academics; that bigger budgets for textbooks and equipment will accomplish anything "if we fail to acknowledge the intellectual ennui that overwhelms our classrooms". It describes a place where kids are now driven all different directions by the mixed messages they get from adult society.

Policy cannot much change the youth culture, the family, society. School needs to adapt to the kids who come. And find a way to get them to learn. Improvements on the present model are unlikely to be enough. Some of the fundamental features of traditional school are almost certainly going to have to change in very significant ways. Jack Frymier's conclusion is likely to be the correct one: Those designing school need to start with what will motivate the students they have.

Frymier spent his career on the curriculum-and-instruction side of public education; as a teacher and administrator, as a professor at the Ohio State University and as a fellow at Phi Delta Kappa. He has not been in the political controversies about reform. His work has been in teaching and learning; with teachers and with kids. It's worth listening carefully to what he said in an education-policy discussion in Minnesota in 1999.

Students have to want to learn

His case is straightforward:

■ Students learn when they're motivated to learn. If they want to learn, they will. If they don't you probably can't make them. Any successful effort to improve learning will therefore need to start with increasing students' motivation.

■ Motivation is an individual matter. Kids differ; in personality, in background and experience, in sociability, in creativity, in intelligence, in their interests. No effort at motivation will succeed unless it works with these differences.[2]

■ School is not very well tuned to the differences in students. Teachers may know kids less well today than in the past. Schools are pressed now to be interested mainly in what kids know and can do; less in who they are. Kids move around, are moved around. Schools are larger: As Ted Sizer has pointed out, high-school teachers especially have far too many students to know any of them well. Schools are also age-graded: Most students are with a teacher for a year; next year, have another. Most discussions about mobility ignore the instability created by this feature of traditional schooling.

■ Curriculum materials are not often adapted to individual students.

■ Teaching methods are not often varied according to the needs and interests of the individual student. Some teachers do this, but many don't. Teachers work mostly with kids in groups. Most are obsessed with classroom management. Most teachers talk too much (as Professor John Goodlad also reported from his research, in A Place Called School).

■ Adapting materials and methods to individual student needs is a teachable skill. This professional practice just isn't very often taught where teachers are trained.

■ Teachers aren't given much opportunity to modify instruction in this way. The curriculum is sequenced; teachers are not encouraged to modify the order in which things are taught or how much time is spent on what. Students are not free to pursue a topic that interests them: The schedule calls for the course to move on.

■ There are few opportunities and few rewards given to teachers for trying to modify teaching in this way, so that learning becomes interesting to the student and becomes the responsibility of the student.

■ It's a mistake for teachers not to favor this. It's much more fun to teach kids who want to learn.

■ Because school takes the form it does, most academic subjects are not of interest to most students, Frymier says: If it weren't for the extracurriculars there would be a revolution by kids in school.

---

[2]There are differences also in aptitude, which is neither intelligence nor interests. The Ball Foundation has developed a test-battery that can distinguish the verbal, abstract, conceptual aptitude from the visual, spatial, tactile. A sense of the importance of aptitudes might guard against the danger that teachers who are themselves verbal, conceptual and abstract will equate this with smart and think of students whose aptitude is visual, spatial, tactile as not-smart.

To motivate students 'school' will have to be different

All this suggests the mismatch between the schools we have and the kind of schools we need if we are to succeed now with all students. And suggests the task we have in bringing the two together.

It clarifies that the problem is not just outside school. The problems in society are real and make a difference: changes in the family, changes in the youth culture. But school is also a part of the problem, failing to do what it could to get all kids learning.

It clarifies that except to the extent schools can get kids to want to learn it may make little difference to introduce standards or to change the learning program. Whatever the standards and whatever the learning program the key in the diverse classrooms of American schools will remain the teacher's ability to adapt the program to motivate the individual student.[3]

And seeing the importance of motivating students clarifies that schools and teachers do carry a responsibility for student performance. Both have long insisted they are not responsible for what the students learn. But they have said they can be and should be accountable for 'best professional practice'. Precisely. Frymier's point is that it is with professional practice that schools are failing. The low student performance is the result, the visible symptom, of this failure.

Too many adults do not relate well to the idea of starting with what interests kids. Many are focused now on improving instruction within the traditional model. Some who favor choice seem not to contemplate choice among the models for learning; envision differences only in governance or ownership. Most have thought of objectives as adults' objectives, and have defined success as the student satisfying the teacher. Many would be uncomfortable with the idea that success should be defined as the teacher meeting the students' needs.

Frymier's argument is not for letting students do whatever they want or against setting standards (though he believes that it is a mistake to drop out things like honesty and responsibility as objectives, and to narrow expectations just to academics). It is simply that as a practical matter kids will not learn unless they are motivated to learn, that the job of schools and teachers is to get them motivated and that if we are serious about all students learning we will have to be serious about arranging school so it does motivate all students. At the moment it does not.

---

[3]At a meeting in California in February 2001 I put Frymier's argument about motivation to a person closely involved with standards-based systemic reform. "I don't buy that", he said. I asked: What will get kids to make the effort required? "We're all working very hard on that", he said. Who is? I asked. He gave me a name at Johns Hopkins. I called that person; put the question to him. "Well", he said, "you have to start with motivation".

What will a 'different' school look like?

It is easy enough to see how school would differ if the design work started with the need to motivate students.

Learning would be individualized. Students would get real scope to pursue their interests. Different students would work on different things. Time would become a variable: Some students would work faster than others; spend more time on some things than on others. At times students would take courses, at times they would not: They would learn by working on projects. Teachers would function less as instructors, more as coaches or advisers. Learning would be less building-bound, less confined to teacher and textbook.

Michael Tillman, a former teacher of the year in Minnesota, likes to say, "Only individualized learning can leave no child behind".

In the period following the Nation at Risk report, Albert Shanker saw clearly this need for school, probably high school especially, to be different. Listen to what the then-president of the American Federation of Teachers said in his weekly column in the Sunday *New York Times* in late May 1988:

> "We all know that every person learns at a different rate. But since most schools organize learning through lectures and set lessons, the students had better learn not at their own rate but at the rate that the teachers present the material. This is, of course, not the teacher's fault: It is what he or she is expected to do. Some students will be bored because they already know it; others will be left behind because they can't move that quickly. Teachers are urged to individualize instruction. The trouble is, in the typical school structure it's almost impossible really to do it.

> "(Individualizing) would give us some idea how to get more than 20 per cent of the kids to learn. If having students listen to lessons and read textbooks doesn't produce the desired result, we need to have other ways of reaching students. While maintaining high goals, we need to try videotapes, audio tapes, computer programs, individual or small-group coaching, peer tutoring, simulation games and trips to various places to get experiences.

> "The way schools are organized now teachers can't do all these things. The teacher is tied down full-time, lecturing to and controlling the class. If we are to reach the 80+ per cent who are not learning now, we'll need to restructure schools so there aren't only one or two methods available to reach kids. We need a system that doesn't blame the kids because the way they actually learn doesn't happen to fit the system's 150-year-old ideas about how kids are supposed to learn."

Three years later Shanker said it again at the Saturn School anniversary in Saint Paul. Because this country does not track kids as some European countries do, the

American teacher is confronted by a mixed-ability classroom. "Learning has got to be individualized," he said. Technology, he could see, is the promise. To avoid humiliating the slower student, to let kids work together, to get away from teacher-talk, to let us avoid tracking. The World Wide Web began to appear only in 1991. Today the web makes it possible to individualize; makes it possible really to have schools organized to motivate students.

The web can make 'school' different

We cannot possibly know at this point what different kinds of schools will appear once the incentives, the rules of the game, are changed. We can, however, get a sense of what might happen by looking at the basic forces moving. The most important of these is surely the recent appearance of the Internet and the web and the extent to which these are now part of young people's life.

Adults are astonished to find how skilled young people are with computers, how good they are at navigating the web. The organization Public Agenda found that college teachers and employers give kids low marks for reading and math but gave them high marks for what they know and can do with computers. Look sometime at a website (in Ireland, actually) that tracks web users: **www.nua.com.**

Teachers have more knowledge about computers than their schools give them scope to use, as Professor Larry Cuban of Stanford University has reported. Still, the kids may also be ahead of most teachers. So there is a question about the common notion that we need, quickly, a catch-up program to train teachers about computers. Perhaps we need, instead, a new way of thinking about school, about learning, that makes real use of the kids' skills and moves both teachers and students into different roles.

In Saint Paul in 2003, in front of the new library under construction for Metropolitan State University, a sign said: Information Access Center. That's worth thinking about. Not so many years ago the information available at the library was in the books available on site. Then with the extensive programs of inter-library loan your library could get users access to books on the shelves of libraries elsewhere. Now with the web, which only appeared, remember, in the early 1990s, the library is an access point for information worldwide. And almost instantly. The books on its shelves are now a small part of what's available at most libraries.

This will be true of school too. Not so long ago the information available on site was what was in the head of the teachers and in the texts and in the books on the school's shelves. Today a student can type a query into a search engine that will scan thousands of servers and report back in less than two seconds. This opens enormous new possibilities for learning. Yet the discussion about learning and teaching is still dominated by the old notion of the teacher as instructor and of information mainly in books.

In traditional school the teacher was the worker. Equipment was minimal: the textbook, the blackboard, the movie projector, the TV set. The technology was group-instruction: students reading and meeting in classes, teachers talking and kids listening, teachers active and kids passive or responding to the teacher's questions.

The appearance of the new equipment, the computers and the internet, cries out for a change in the technology of learning. Understand: To an economist the capital is not the technology. The computers, the connections, the net and the web are capital, and technology is the way capital and labor are combined. The assembly line was a new technology because it was a different way of combining capital and labor, a radical reorganization of work.

The Internet and web require us to change the technology of school. It is not a matter of adding the computer, the server, the Internet connections to the present teacher-directed classroom. The new learning materials of computer, Internet and web imply a fundamental change in the way teachers and students relate to each other—students more active and purposeful, the teacher in a new role as adviser, guide and coach—individualizing education. It has the potential to make learning more relevant, more interesting and more motivating for kids. And more rewarding and enjoyable for teachers.

It could also, not incidentally, help in important ways with the economic unsustainability of the traditional labor-intensive technology that uses teachers so largely to present material to students.

Two different meanings of 'different'

We have been talking here, and will be talking more, about different schools and new schools and about creating different schools new. It will be well to clarify the terms before talking further about what the states should do. Words matter. Old terms lock people into old concepts. If we want to think about new concepts then the terms must be clear.

In what follows 'different' will have two meanings.

▪ Different from the standard schooling today

Earlier chapters have described traditional schooling, with its traditional technologies and their traditional student and teacher roles. These concepts should change and are bound to change.

New and better methods of teaching elementary-school children how to read are appearing. The web will increasingly give secondary-school students access to information directly, individualizing learning and disintermediating the teacher in a way that improves student motivation and permits students to move at different speeds. New schools will be created that use these new and different methods.

But the idea is not just to find some one different and better kind of school. It is not a search for a new best way, to replace the current "one best way" for all kids.

■ *Different from each other, reflecting differences among kids*

'Different schools' also means schools different from each other. Students differ in readiness, in aptitude, in motivation, in the rate at which they can learn. School needs to fit to, needs to adapt to, these differences. There will need to be many new kinds of school.

Think about transportation. Riding is different than walking; faster and more comfortable. But we would not be satisfied with just one kind of vehicle even if superior to walking. Different families have different needs; different tasks require different vehicles. It is good to have sedans and light trucks and semi-trailers and motorcycles and even SUVs to choose among.

I know a person who went through high school with 4,000 others and thought it was wonderful. Other kids are lost in a school that large. College-prep is right for some, not for others. Some kids will learn well listening to teachers, others will learn better if they can work at their own pace on subjects of real interest to them. If motivation is indeed the key, then some schools might need to offer students the opportunity to learn while earning money in a workplace.

It is a struggle to maintain a diversity of opportunity for students against the insistence of some adults that, no, there is only one right kind of learning and so only one right kind of school. To break through this deadlock it will be helpful to listen to the students. Up to now students have not had much voice in the discussion about their education.

Two different ways to get different schools

It's worth putting into focus again, too, the different ways that state policy can produce different schools: trying simply to get existing schools to change, and trying to create different schools new.

■ *Making the existing different: transformation*

When dealing with inanimate things we accept that the existing cannot change into something substantially different. We can replace the planking and the rigging and the decking of a boat so it will be 'like new', but it will be the same boat with the same performance characteristics. We can alter it somewhat in rebuilding it, so that its performance marginally improves. But if we want a substantially different boat we have to buy a different one, or design and build a different boat new.

Interestingly, when we talk about human organizations we assume the existing can dramatically change, like that caterpillar transforming itself into a butterfly. The managers of the organization tell us they can lead major change. Our impulse is to believe them. 'Believe' becomes the operable word. So all the chips are bet on this transformation, through leadership, driven by 'requirements'.

But when a senior official with the New York City schools told a meeting in California in 2001 that the city was going to convert the entire operation the next year to some new computerized procedure the CEO of an electronics company told him, "No, you're not. You may think you can do that. But you're talking about people changing their behavior in really significant ways. I am sorry if this offends central management, but you cannot make people change their behavior." And he went on to describe the experience of the Internet-related firms in California. You bring in the new technology. Some people will use it; some will not. You work with those who will. In time others will. The new practice becomes established, the change happens. But gradually.

States have been trying for years to help districts change the schools they have.

Reducing and even repealing regulations was an early and obvious idea. At one point the Minnesota Legislature offered to waive all its regulations for a district that was interested in being innovative and was willing to be accountable. Legislators found, however, that the districts' tendency to complain about overregulation was in no way matched by their willingness to use the freedoms made available as regulations were withdrawn.

It is hard to get new practice to spread. Removing-regulations and disseminating-best-practice were widely tried. They are generally discredited as strategies for significant change. Altering the existing is not a promising way to change existing operations very significantly, very quickly. And when districts do create different schools the differences may not last. When she became superintendent in Robbinsdale, Minn., Donna Carter created a Technology Learning Center. Initially veteran teachers chose not to move there. As the school proved successful and popular the veteran teachers began to bump in. "Month by month", Carter said just before leaving for California, "I watch it becoming more like every other school we have."

■ Creating the different new: Replacement

If we need something substantially different it is better to acquire something that is already different or to create something different new. This is common wisdom.

Some time back I flew into New York after not having been there for several years. When I'd seen it last from the air it was a blue city with mercury-vapor street lights. Now, looking out the left side of the plane over northern New Jersey, it was a gold city. A stunning change. But the mercury-vapor lights had not changed into low-sodium lights. Pole by pole, street by street, neighborhood by neighborhood the mercury-vapor lights had been replaced with low-sodium lights.

With respect to organizations, too, starting-new may be the best way to get the different and better model we need. As Joe Graba puts it, not many people thinking of starting an airline went about it by trying to transform a railroad. Education has been an exception: The discussion has been almost entirely about getting the better by transforming the existing. We need to be open to some notion of replacement, of arranging for new and better schools gradually to take the place of existing schools that do not improve. As this process of replacement proceeds the institution changes.

For these different schools to appear, as we will see in Chapter 7, the K-12 institution itself will need to change. We will need a variety of entities to produce the variety of different schools.

It cannot be done just by the existing district. People who come together in an organization tend to believe in a best way, tend to have a common view of how things should be done. It is hard to accommodate a number of divergent philosophies within a single structure of governance and management. Some educators argue even that the standardization must extend across all schools, so students who move will find the same program in any school into which they transfer. But this is not France and students are not all alike. Strategically, to make available the necessary variety of learning methods in the face of the internal pressure for uniformity, it was essential for state policy leadership to withdraw the exclusive; to let more than one organization offer public education in the community, to have different kinds of schools appear and to make it possible for students then to choose.

The diversity of organizations will speed innovation, stimulating the development of still other new methods of learning. The wisdom in the telephone industry is instructive: that "Innovation always moves faster between organizations than within them".

So: What should state leadership do?

The more attractive the potential the more urgent the question about method, about how to realize the potential. The next chapters will examine the two methods available: Changing existing schools and creating different schools new. Chapter 6 reviews the new situation created for districts as the states moved to require student performance and withdrew the 'exclusive franchise'. Chapter 7 will look at ways to enable the districts to respond to this new situation. Chapter 8 considers why the states should also create new organizations to start new schools, and how that can be done. Chapter 9 looks at some intriguing examples of new schools, secondary schools appearing in Minnesota and in Milwaukee that are different from traditional schools in their governance as well as in their learning model.

Chapter 6

KEEP PRESSING THE DISTRICTS TO CHANGE AND IMPROVE

The theory has been that districts will improve their schools if standards are set, if performance is measured and if they are somehow held accountable for their schools' improvement. So far so good: The pressure is important.

Increasingly after the national law in 2002, however, its implementation became tangled in arguments about how to get there, in the details in which as people say the devil resides. And tangled, predictably, in objections that the districts cannot make the required changes and improvements unless the state gives them more money—an objection which both then pass on to the national government.

So the country is struggling to make the transition from a static, inert institution to a dynamic, self-improving institution. It has commanded the institution to do better, but not yet really figured out how that is to happen.

State policy leadership is working pragmatically along two lines, with practice running ahead of theory.

■ It has been setting the standards—required now by the national legislation—for what students should know and be able to do, and how well. And introducing measurements of performance and some consequences for not making 'adequate' improvements in performance.

■ It has also—though not required by national legislation—been withdrawing the district's exclusive on public education in the community, opening the way for other entities to offer public education in the community, creating different schools new and in the process broadening the choices available for parents and students.

In this chapter we will look briefly at these two system changes and at how they can be most effective.

State policy has delivered a double 'shock'

The introduction of accountability and the withdrawal of the exclusive were a shock to the K-12 institution.

Districts and schools needed a shock to cause them to take seriously the national sense of the need for improvement; needed something that changed the rules of the game in ways that removed their ability to put the interests of their adult members ahead of the interests of the students and of the public.[1]

For years the states were in default on this responsibility. But after about 1985 they began putting their districts and schools under pressure for performance, removing the guarantee of district success whether or not the students learned.

Accountability has been the more visible effort, has been pushed the furthest. The country is a very long way from being finished with the discussion about what students should know and be able to do. And about how to measure student and school performance. Also, about consequences: what to do—and to whom—if students and schools fail to perform. But the commitment to student learning seems firmly set, as does the idea that the system should provide for keeping score and that something should depend, for someone, on whether the students learn.

The effort to withdraw the exclusive gets less support, is less developed. But in most states policy is continuing to make it possible for somebody other than the local board to offer public education in the community, supplementing choice with choic/es. Partly states have given students the opportunity to enroll in the district next door, partly they have acted through the chartering laws to give somebody else the opportunity to start schools where the students live.

On this question, too, the country has a lot of thinking left to do. The present chartering laws are not the only way to arrange for the new choic/es to be made available. But with the new-schools effort, as with accountability, the policy breakthrough has been made. The exclusive has been withdrawn. The question now is what other entities will be designated to offer public education and how many of these there will be.

Both of these are radical changes in the traditional system givens. Let's consider each, in turn.

Performance is now measured and reported

Until quite recently student learning was not an imperative.

This sounds strange to say, but in truth, as Dan Loritz put it when he was deputy chief of staff for Minnesota Gov. Rudy Perpich, the state was "in the opportunity

---

[1] On the notion of a shock as a necessary stimulus to innovation within an organization see Andrew Van de Ven et al, *The Innovation Journey*, Oxford University Press, New York 1999.

business". The state required kids to attend, from ages 7 to 16. And it required the districts to offer a minimum set of subjects which kids had to take. If kids learned, well and good. But the state did not insist they learn. Clearly it did not, since it did not check, did not measure student learning. And while life might impose some consequences on students who did not learn, the state imposed none directly; not on the student and not on the school or district.

This is now changing fundamentally as national and state policy introduce standards, measurement and consequences. But it has not been easy to make this accountability model work. One or two of the elements can be implemented fairly easily: The trick is to get all three operating together, especially when—in the absence of national standards—each state decides how rigorous each element will be. This difficulty was clearly visible by 2004 in the backpressure from states and districts against No Child Left Behind.

■ *Standards, Testing, Consequences*

Several questions run through the debate about standards. One is whether the public, the government, should set standards at all. Another is about the level of government that should set them: state, local, national. A third is what the standards should require.

The first and second seem broadly agreed: There will be standards, and they will be set by the states. Debate continues about the concept of learning that should be written into them. The conventional phrasing that says standards are about "what students should know and be able to do" works for elementary school: No one disagrees that young children should be able to read and write, count and compute. The debate has mainly to do with the standards for secondary school, for teenagers. Here the notion of 'be able to do' is dominated by the notion that students should 'know' the subject-matter of each academic discipline. Chapter 10 will return to the question of what the states' approach to standards ought to be.

The arrival of accountability intensifies also the debate about measurement and consequences.

The 2002 national legislation raised the question whether testing should measure student performance relative to some absolute level or should measure gains; 'value added', from whatever level. Though the law says 'all children' strong arguments are heard that not all students are ready to learn and that not all schools and districts are ready to teach. So, predictably, there are protests from districts whose students start farther behind.

This quickly entangles the discussion in issues of equity and in arguments that standards and consequences cannot fairly be imposed until resources have been provided to make the students and the schools 'ready'. Also, in an argument that if standards are introduced they should be set at different levels for students at different levels of achievement or ability. Others disagree with that, arguing it is wrong to expect less of low-performing students.

There are complicated questions about testing. How high should the pass-rate be set? Should performance be related to goals or to standards? How far can the standard be set below the goal, and how far may acceptable performance fall short of the standard? Is testing a mechanism for accountability? Or is it a diagnostic tool for teachers? Is it OK or not-OK to teach (to) the test? Where only certain subjects are tested what is lost from the educational experience? Is the present level of testing appropriate or is it out of control, stimulating a competition among students that is destructive of learning and that will in fact reduce what students know and are able to do?

The arguments over standards and measurement complicate the decision about what exactly the consequences are to be. What is fair? On whom are the consequences to fall? Just on the students? Or on adults in the schools as well?

The traditional notion has been that it is only students who fail: "We have a system without consequences for failure," Howard Fuller told the Milwaukee board when he came in as superintendent, "in which everyone is protected except the children." But inescapably there will be consequences for adults if testing reveals low performance.

Schools and teachers feel stigmatized if their school is labeled low-performing or is put on probation. If they are going to be held accountable, they are inclined to say, they should be able to make more of the decisions that help determine whether and how well their students learn.

Board members have reason to fear that accountability will fall on them whether they centralize or decentralize decisions. They are the only officials that parents have the power to remove. They worry about the political consequences for themselves if too many kids fail: Parents do not enroll their children not to get a diploma. So boards might be reluctant to impose consequences at all, or might try to get the state to ease up on standards or on pass-rates.

Resistance is growing

Through 2003 and 2004 a variety of objections produced a growing resistance to the accountability model. States resented the way it was imposed. Districts objected to the costs it would generate, complaining that these are "not fully funded". Others questioned the realism of requiring high performance from all children in special education or those just learning English, and of expecting very small districts to staff the full range of high school courses with 'highly qualified teachers'. There are concerns, too, about 'adequate yearly progress': about the base from which this is measured, about the acceptable rate of progress; about the definition of 'progress' and about the growing number of districts likely to be tagged as not making adequate yearly progress.

It is not quite clear how far the stated objections are the real objections and how far they are a cover for an underlying resistance on the part of districts—and of teachers and their unions—to being held accountable at all, especially for the performance of 'sub-groups' broken out by race and reported separately.

In response to these objections the national administration made a few adjustments, but—perhaps feeling that the objections were not so much 'We can't' as they were 'We don't want to'—kept these to a minimum. Nor did its political opposition press too hard, so many of its own leading figures having voted for No Child Left Behind.

The resistance was building out in the states, where in a number of legislatures moves were made to direct the state department of education not to comply; even to reject the federal aid, as a way of shedding the requirements attached to it. In some cases—as in Minnesota—the effort brought together liberal Democrats and conservative Republicans, united in their opposition even if for different reasons. Administration spokespersons were flying around the country, trying to damp down the smoldering opposition.

Beyond this, and perhaps more important, there is some genuine opposition even to things that appear on the surface to be agreed-on.

This has mainly to do with the way student performance and the elements of the accountability model are defined. Essentially the concern is that consequences related to scores on tests, tests mainly of items subject to recall and standards mainly about course content, will work actually to narrow what students know and are able to do. As a big-city superintendent put it at a meeting in Boston in April 2004: "My concern is that while scores are going up, learning is going down". A well-known supporter of standards told me that this concern is widespread among college and university presidents—none of whom will speak out publicly. They are not the only persons afraid to raise questions, fearful of being accused of 'being against standards'.

So one concern is that Congress is likely to take up the less significant questions when it begins to amend No Child Left Behind rather than the fundamental questions that more urgently need to be discussed.

Will raising standards really lift performance?

Questions do need to be raised. The theory was that raising standards would pull performance up. Some in the discussion seem to assume that setting standards is enough, that the threat of serious consequences will by itself drive students to meet whatever standards are set. In some discussions you almost get a sense that people believe that once standards are set and accountability is clear, all students will get 'A's in all courses.

The accountability model says that students who fail to learn will not move ahead or will not graduate. But remember, as teachers have told us: School can't make kids learn. It can't even make kids attend, and after age 16 most don't have to attend. Whether they attend, whether they work hard, is up to them. If students aren't there, or don't try, then standards and the threat of being held back in grade or of not graduating will not raise performance. It will simply drive up the quit-rate.

And if too many students do not meet standards and are failed there will be a problem, as boards and legislatures understand. Realistically, how many students can a district fail? Fail too many and students and their parents will rebel. Then the standards (or the passing-mark) might be lowered enough to make the failure-rate tolerable. Through 2003 the education press carried story after story about districts or states modifying the tests, adjusting the cut-scores or putting off the effective date for the consequences to take effect.

Suppose the theory were recast to say that performance drives standards. Let's say standards can be kept, politically, five percent above the level of performance. Then the way to raise standards will be to raise performance. The better the students do, the higher the standards can be set.

To raise performance we should first enlarge the capacity of schools to get kids to want to learn. The fear of not getting a diploma may give students a reason to learn. But that may not be enough. You can tell a high school boy he will not graduate if he cannot jump chest-height (which is about the standard for that age). But threatening him does not teach him. The threat might be a part of motivating him. But still school has to interest students enough to cause them to attend and to work hard and to learn well. If it does then performance will rise and standards can be raised.

The idea of standards is now locked onto the public's sense of the need for improvement. But the country has a long way to go yet to think through the questions about standards not solved in the 2002 legislation; especially, how to reconcile the desire for accountability and the desire for flexibility. Again: this is a question to which we will return in Chapter 10.[2]

The state has withdrawn the 'exclusive'

The district traditionally had an exclusive on public education within its boundaries. So did the school: You probably went to the grade school and high school that served your 'attendance area'.

---

[2]See page 123.

In the 1960s the school attendance area began to disappear. Where a district adopted a desegregation plan, students were offered some choice: usually another neighborhood school or a magnet school. In the 1970s Minneapolis was an all-choice district. The district would not assign a student anywhere. Every family had to choose.

This intra-district choice—involving only its own schools—did not put the district at risk. And in truth did not put even its schools much at risk. Parents who found their first-choice school full were offered their second choice, or third. What actually happened were waiting lists. The district was slow to expand sought-after programs. Some districts were proud of their waiting lists. Intra-district choice was not a program to press the schools for improvement, not an effort to close schools that did not improve.

Then in the 1980s state interventions began to withdraw the exclusive from the district. Students could choose to enroll in other districts, or with some other learning organization that was not part of a local district. Suddenly the district of residence was no longer the only organization authorized to offer public education to those within its borders. This was a radical change in the traditional system givens, and was to a degree intended to generate pressure for improvement. Frustrated by the unresponsiveness of the districts the states, with these laws opening education to "somebody else who will", were trying to create dynamics for the districts by creating new opportunities for the students.

■ Colleges and universities may offer 11th and 12th grades

With its Post-secondary Option, authored by then-Rep. Connie Levi in 1985, Minnesota made it possible for 11th- and 12th-graders to enroll full- or part-time in universities and colleges within the state and to earn credit toward both high school and college graduation at the same time, fully at public expense.

Fearful of the districts' reaction the colleges and universities did not openly recruit. But students told each other about the opportunity. Enrollment quickly rose to about five per cent of the eligibles. The students did well. And the districts quickly responded; offering college-in-the-school and similar programs to hold enrollment in the high school.

■ Other districts may enroll the students

Gov. Rudy Perpich in Minnesota had proposed inter-district open enrollment, too, in 1985. This program came into law and operation in 1988–89. It proved slow going. Reluctant to enroll each others' students the districts found ways to frustrate inter-district choice by closing to non-residents, pointing to lack of space as enrollments grew.

Open enrollment was limited also by the similarity among districts. "Why would students want to move?" one superintendent asked in a discussion in the early '80s. "Ninety per cent of our curriculum is the same." This stimulated policy thinking about other ways to generate different schools.

■ *Others may now 'charter' new schools*

With inter-district enrollment and the post-secondary option the states made it possible for entities other than the resident district to enroll students in their existing courses and classes. The option to choose was new. But the schools of the 'somebody else' were not.

Then in the '90s many states made it possible also for others to create new schools for students wanting to move. These were the laws authorizing the chartering of new public schools designed and proposed by teachers and others.

From the start the idea was that chartering would not be limited to the local board. And as the idea spread across the country the laws gradually broadened the range of non-district organizations authorized to sponsor. The state board of education was added in some states, post-secondary institutions in some states. In some cases a law created an entirely new organization to authorize the new schools: Arizona's State Board for Charter Schools, for example. In 1995 the Congress as legislature for the District of Columbia created the D.C. Public Charter Schools Board.

In Minnesota's initial 1991 charter law chartering was limited to the local board of education, as it is still in some states. In this form the law essentially provides a way for the district itself to broaden its own offerings through the chartering of new schools; a way for the district to respond to the pressures for change and improvement created by the state's accountability pressure. Chapter 7 will consider further this opportunity for the district to use the chartering laws.

■ *The courts are opening the door to non-public schools*

There has been a long discussion also about a 'voucher' program, about the idea of the public paying for students to enroll in non-public schools. For years there was more discussion than action. Proposals were voted on and defeated in a number of states, both in legislatures and in referenda. But in the 1990s legislatures in Wisconsin and Ohio acted, creating programs for Milwaukee and for Cleveland. In Florida in 1999 the Legislature made this a choice for students statewide in schools that do not succeed.

Further action waited on clearing away the constitutional objections. Proponents sought a test case, and the Cleveland program was challenged. In July 2002 the United States Supreme Court found the Cleveland program constitutional.

Everyone seemed conscious, afterward, how many hurdles remain for the idea, in state courts and in state legislatures. But in 2003 a small program was enacted in

Colorado. And early in 2004 Congress enacted a limited program for the District of Columbia. Even if small these are additional steps in the process of system change, in the unbundling of the traditional institution.

Will districts respond to the shock?

Introducing accountability has had a real impact on the institution. The districts are sensitive to the way the testing and the reporting of scores has made the public and the media aware of how far the institution has to go to get students — certain groups of students, particularly — up to the level at which they should and could be performing. Districts feel embarrassed, feel pressure. They are now leaning hard on their schools and teachers to raise scores.

Similarly, districts have felt the loss of their exclusive, the loss of students to the new schools chartered. For the districts the removal of their exclusive was unexpected. They were surprised by how quickly these laws spread across the country and by the ability and the willingness of the elected policy leadership in virtually every major state to enact these laws over the opposition of the K-12 associations. Districts now watch the new learning programs appearing, feel the students moving and taking their money with them. They feel a little of the pressure that the chartered schools themselves feel, the sense that there is now increasingly a 'have to'.

Yet the districts have been slow to respond to these system changes. Mostly districts have been trying to get scores up within the framework of traditional school without much changing the program of learning or the concepts of schooling. And in most states the districts have been trying rather more to block the creation of new schools than to use the chartering laws to create new and improved schools themselves.

Accountability and the withdrawal of the exclusive give districts a reason to improve. And for some districts having a reason may be enough to cause at least modest adjustments in the program.[3]

Some districts seeing 11th- and 12th-graders moving into college under a post-secondary option introduced college-level programs in their high schools. If a chartered school appeared offering all-day kindergarten the district often added all-day kindergarten. When the chartered sector appeared with its small schools the long

---

[3]The new choices, the new schools chartered by others, will not and cannot themselves change or improve the district's schools. There has been a somewhat careless discussion about a 'ripple effect', the analogy of a pebble dropped in a pool creating rings. A moment's reflection shows the error. The analogy assumes the water is liquid. If the pond is frozen, no ripple. Similarly: Whether the district schools change when a chartered school is dropped into the community depends on the district. Only the district can change district schools.

discussion about smaller schools became serious: A number of districts with grants from the Gates Foundation began to break their big high schools into small learning communities.

But these are modest adjustments. Districts can always add incrementally to their program, spending more to do so. The important question is whether they can change what goes on in existing schools dramatically enough as new schools, created by others, begin to appear. The question is partly the districts' willingness to do so, partly their capacity to do so. Change is hard within the existing framework of ownership, employment and the master contract. The high schools especially have been almost intractable, everywhere.

Perhaps the shock to the district is not enough. Perhaps the states need to give the districts the ability to use the chartering laws to create different schools, as a way to increase the districts' own capacity to improve.

This is becoming a basic policy question for the states.

Chapter 7

ENLARGE THE DISTRICTS' CAPACITY TO CREATE NEW SCHOOLS

As the states open the institution to new schools created by others, the states should in fairness increase the districts' capacity to create new schools themselves.

A district that uses this new opportunity will have to think in a new way. It will have to get out of the old public-utility mentality, out of the notion that the only schools that are its schools are those the district owns and runs, and out of the notion that it has to be an employer. A board that stops thinking of itself as a 'school board' and begins to think of itself as an 'education board', responsible for arranging learning opportunities for students, will find its capacity enlarged. It will also have extricated itself from the conflict of interest created by its dual role as policymaker and as operator.

A district board may or may not decide it wants to do this. But it should have the opportunity to do so if it wishes.

So it will be useful now to consider how the state can make it increasingly possible for a district to function as an education board. In Chapter 12 we will come back to the question of how likely districts are to use that authority if it is made available to them.

Districts do start some new schools

Districts do create new schools, of course. When enrollments are growing a developing suburban district may build a new school every few years. But this is not what we mean here by 'new'. These schools will probably be much like existing schools in their program, in their governance, even in their architecture. They are new but not different.

Districts do create some new schools that are different. Boards and superintendents typically want to show the community that the district is open to different approaches to learning that the public has heard about. So often this-or-that program will appear.

But these schools, like the new-and-not-different, continue to be owned and operated by the district. Schools truly 'different' are schools that have different approaches to learning and that are substantially autonomous; not owned and operated by the board. This different governance is essential for real change.

Schools different both in their program and in their governance have appeared as district 'alternative' schools.

Most different schools have been 'alternative' schools

Quietly, without attracting much attention, districts began in the early 1970s to set up schools for the growing number of non-traditional students, for kids "not doing well" in the traditional school setting. Not much has been written about this new sector of district public education: *Education Week* has barely covered it; the Education Commission of the States has barely researched it. It is a dark continent of American public education.

It is usually a surprise even to well-informed people and to most journalists to be told how large this sector has become. In Minnesota the alternative schools were by 2002 handling over 100,000 students in the course of a year; perhaps a quarter of all secondary students.[1]

The alternative schools often do things the districts do not typically do in their regular schools. They sometimes operate on different schedules. They may operate year-round. They may take different approaches to learning. Most often kids are referred, but some are schools of choice. Most are owned and operated by the districts, but in some cases these schools are nonprofit organizations contracted to the district, hiring their own teachers outside the district master agreement. Sometimes even where run by the district these schools may select their own teachers and have their own seniority system. Sometimes they operate in leased, private space. Some schools look different. I remember the school in South St. Paul where the students had draped cloth to cover the glare from the ceiling industrial lighting and had brought in floor lamps they'd bought at some second-hand store to set by their tables.

The states can and in some cases do help by enacting a state framework within which districts can create these schools. Minnesota did this with its Area Learning Centers law in 1985. In Wisconsin the districts have used the charter law mainly to create alternative schools.

---

[1] To see "Alternative Education Programs, the Quiet Giant in Minnesota Public Education" go to **www.EducationEvolving.org.**

It is generally understood: The district grants this atypical autonomy because these alternative schools take the kids the traditional schools cannot handle or do not want. The late Jim Boyle, a former public school principal in Illinois who started Ombudsman, Inc. as a for-profit contractor to districts, used to tell about the day a principal presented him to the teachers' meeting. "I'm going to read a list of the students who will not be in your classes next fall," the principal said. And he read the list. The room applauded. "Now," the principal said, "let me introduce the man who is the reason why these students will not be in your classes next fall."

By the 1980s the alternative-school educators were forming associations in many states. Like the students, the educators in this sector are a rather different lot. The sector seems to attract teachers and administrators who had long advocated non-traditional ways of educating kids, who had been frustrated, who were perhaps regarded as 'troublemakers' themselves in the district setting. Some had been in the 'lab' schools run by colleges of education and came into alternative education when the lab school was closed in the 1970s.[2]

An affiliation of state associations began holding annual national meetings about 1990. These were remarkably happy meetings; full of people who felt good about the challenge of taking the toughest kids even with less money, when given the freedom to do things differently. Leaders of the Minnesota Association of Alternative Programs have recently been trying to form a national association.

The sector deserves more attention than it has received. As the pressure for performance causes districts to refer more and more low-performing students it is likely to continue to grow. But this new sector is limited as a strategy for change. It is the district doing something different only for 'different' kids. And the 'admissions requirement' is to fail in regular school. Something else, something more, is clearly required to produce the range of options needed for the mainline student population.

Boards might contract for schools run by others

Some states have tried to give boards the authority to acquire (or to create) a new and different school through contract. The contract might be with either a non-profit or a for-profit vendor. A board could buy a single school or several, from a single operator or from several. It could buy the whole operation, or just the management of the operation, or just the learning program.

This should improve both autonomy and accountability. Contract arrangements inherently force attention to objectives, measurement and consequences in

[2]Lab schools were closed partly because they were a charge the colleges could no longer afford and partly because their function (at times) as schools for the children of university faculty attracted the opposition of the teachers union and its legislative supporters. Asked to define University High, which he had run for the College of Education at the University of Minnesota, Dean William Gardner said: "It was a public school that operated on private-school principles". Conversation with the author.

ways that administrative, bureau arrangements do not. If I am going to sign an agree-ment to do a job for you, we will both want to be clear what it is I am expected to accomplish. We will want to be sure we have a way to know whether I have done the job satisfactorily. And each of us will want to be able to hold the other account-able, for performance and for payment. Most boards and top managers will be, can be, tougher with a contractor than with their own employees.

Contract arrangements are not without problems; patronage and corruption are not unknown. But there are problems in the public-bureau arrangement as well. The bureau arrangement in K-12 is essentially a sole-source, non-competitive, cost-plus, indefinitely-renewable contract. Someone suggested to Ruth Randall when she was Minnesota's commissioner of education that if the commissioner of trans-portation bought road construction the way the commissioner of education 'buys' schooling s/he could be prosecuted, tried, convicted and punished.

Contract arrangements are common in the public sector outside K-12. Man-agement often uses other organizations to carry out agency purposes, in order to avoid having to own and run, itself, everything it is required to do. Contrary to the common impression, contracting by a governmental body is not privatization. Someone else may do the work, but the public purpose remains.[3] Contracting is also common in the private sector. A few examples make the point.

Airports—At the Twin Cities International Airport on any given day there will be almost 18,000 people working. Perhaps 500 of them work for the Metropolitan Airports Commission, the public body responsible for Lindbergh Terminal. The other workers, in the terminal and on the ground side, work for the airlines and for other organizations providing food, books, coffee, security, insurance, auto-rental, taxi, maintenance and other services. The public agency is essentially a manager of contracts.

Child day care—Minnesota has a large and growing program of public child care that is run through county government. But the counties do not own and oper-ate the child-care centers. And they do not want to. Their concept of running the program is a concept of buying service. They determine eligibility for subsidy, con-tract with both child-care centers and family day care providers and pay the con-tractors for service. County managers believe they can focus better on objectives and on performance—which means, increasingly, on child development—if they do not own the facilities and employ the staff. Even in the county social service offices that offer child care, the service is bought-in.

---

[3]See Ted Kolderie, "The Two Different Concepts of Privatization", *Public Administration Review*, July/August 1986. This difference between deciding and doing, between making policy and running operations, was David Osborne's distinction between 'steering' and 'rowing' in *Reinventing Government*, Addison Wesley, 1992.

Transportation—In almost any state the highway department (now Department of Transportation) will be a very large purchase-of-service operation. Its roads are commonly built and sometimes even maintained on contract, and a large body of wisdom about how to buy smart has built up in these organizations.

Retail stores—Ask your local department store or, increasingly, supermarket about its leased departments. You will learn that, while these are designed so the customer cannot tell the difference, some departments of the store are in fact not owned by the company that owns the store. Experience has taught the company that others can do some things better than it can do them. So fine jewelry often, books sometimes, oriental rugs, optical, photo labs, flowers and other departments are run in the store by some other business; sometimes a local firm, sometimes a major corporation.

It is interesting to sit educators down for an evening with someone who knows leased operations. In short order people are thinking: "We could organize a high school like this!"

Most important, boards can use their option to charter

The charter laws have been the states' main effort to help districts create different schools new. These laws now exist in workable form in about 25 states, and local boards may use them in every chartering state but Massachusetts and New Jersey (where chartering is a state function). The laws let boards create schools they do not have to run, schools that can be closed if they do not work. Boards can concentrate on policy: What kind of learning program do we want? How much are we going to spend? What organizations should we bring in to run the schools? How well are they performing?

The case for district chartering was never made better than by Randy Quinn, then executive secretary of the Colorado Association of School Boards (CASB), in the association magazine in August 1993.

The association, he noted, had opposed the charter-schools bill supported by Governor Roy Romer and authored by Rep. Peggy Kerns and Sen. Bill Owens (who would succeed Romer as governor). CASB first tried to modify the bill, Quinn wrote. When this failed they tried to kill it—and failed again. So, he asked: "Now what? Is it the beginning of the end of public education?" No, he decided. But the board's role will change. The traditional role has been to hire teachers, administrators and other staff, he noted. Schools granted charter status will become in large measure self-governing. The board becomes in effect the purchaser of education services on behalf of the community.

"This opens up all kinds of possibilities." A board could identify its needs for new education programs, then use the chartering process to implement those programs in new schools, monitoring performance to be sure the school does the job well. It could use the law to place its programs in other facilities, perhaps in a corporate work site as a convenience to employees. And chartering could help the board out of difficult arguments about what the district schools should or should not do; help it escape the assumption that all schools must follow a single philosophy. It would make it easier to create a distinctive school outside the district administration for those who want another kind of education for their children.

Quinn concluded: "Colorado school boards would be well advised to tap their creative insight to examine how this new concept can best serve their communities' children. . . Moving away from the role of exclusive (operator) of education services may be a blessing in disguise."[4]

Chartering can combine with contracting. The chartered school is almost everywhere a non-profit corporation (or its equivalent). Non-profits may enter into contracts. So an opportunity exists for a chartered school to buy its learning program rather than to set up and run the program itself. Nationally perhaps about 15 percent of the chartered schools do contract either for the learning program or for the management of it. For a district, doing contracting through chartering avoids the problems that come with trying to connect directly to a commercial vendor. The non-profit in between is a kind of cartilege, cushioning what would otherwise be bone-on-bone.

Early on, the firms offering to run schools spotted the charter sector as an emerging market: Edison Schools, Mosaica, National Heritage Academies, Chancellor Beacon Academies, Charter Schools USA and other companies selling learning programs. This has helped make the chartered sector even more an 'R&D sector' of American public education.

Realistically, can the districts create an open sector?

Districts have been slow to use the new opportunities that state policy leadership has provided them, both to let their owned schools be truly different and to create new schools. There are two ways to go into a cold lake. You can wade in slowly. Or you can run down the dock and leap off. Down the beach are the schools in the chartered sector, running and leaping in. The districts have been wading in slowly.

Randy Quinn's argument—that chartering is a way for the board to solve some of its most difficult problems—was a hard sell to member boards in Colorado. It is not common, anywhere, for a board to do what the board did in Duluth, Minn., and

---

[4]After someone had sent me the column I called Quinn. I asked: How did you come to this? Is it something you'd always believed, and just now have the opportunity to say? No, he said. "I began to see it during the legislative debate."

in Wilkinsburg, Pa.: to run a national competition for good learning models, pick the best design and charter or contract with a nonprofit organization then to operate it.

Where boards have sponsored schools it is often not out of a conviction that this was the way for the district itself to change and improve. Sometimes it is to offload a short-term peak of staffing and facility expense, or because someone else would sponsor the school if the board did not—the feeling being that if the school is going to appear anyway "We would rather have some control of it". So the experience to date is not encouraging.

Various big-city districts have been talking about going into chartering; about having internally an open sector alongside the schools the board owns and operates. Chicago is; Philadelphia is; New York City is; San Diego is; Buffalo, N.Y., is; Los Angeles may still be.[5] This always presents problems. Some in the district administration may not like the freedom afforded to the not-owned schools. And there is almost always an objection from the teachers union, which is unlikely to want the board to charter schools whose teacher-employees may not choose to unionize. A requisite for the success of a district open sector may be to find a way to make the new-schools program compatible with the interests of the union—as in Milwaukee where teachers are chartered to be responsible for the school while remaining district employees and under the master contract.[6]

Where the district will not or cannot create an open sector it should perhaps accept that its best role is to concentrate on running the traditional schools in which middle-class parents are happy, and to let others set up and run the new and different schools for kids not doing well in traditional school. The job for the state will then be to arrange for that 'somebody else'. The groups concerned that their kids are doing poorly should then focus on state rather than district action.

Chapter 8, next, explains the strategy emerging in the states to expand the K-12 institution beyond the district organizations. Chapter 11 will consider the objections that governors and legislators are encountering and will have to overcome as they work this radical change in system arrangements. It is never easy to change old and settled ways of thinking. Successful politicians, though, are usually good educators. So there is hope.

---

[5]In July 2004 Chicago Mayor Richard Daley proposed 100 new schools; a third contract, a third chartered, a third created by the city. A national overview of open sectors appearing can be found on **www.EducationEvolving.org**.

[6]See Chapter 9.

Chapter 8

CREATE NEW ENTITIES TO AUTHORIZE NEW SCHOOLS

The slowness of the districts to change existing schools is a concern for legislators and governors. The states are under an imperative to improve both student and school performance. They cannot accept an assertion from the districts that change can proceed only as fast as the districts find it comfortable to proceed. If the district sector does not—cannot or will not—produce the schools we need then the states will have to get somebody else who will.

State policy leadership does have that option. The institution and its system, the rules of the game, are in state law. Governors and legislatures can change both the institution and the principles on which it is built. The states need to use that option, in their own interest and in the public interest.

This will put the states on a dual track toward improvement: continuing to do whatever can be done to improve existing schools while also creating new entities that will create different and better schools new.

In truth, state policy leadership is well begun on the creation of a new, open sector of public education outside the district framework. Governors and legislatures know how to do this and know how to expand it. What they need to know next is how to defend this radical change in traditional arrangements, how to explain clearly and persuasively why a one-bet strategy that tries only to change existing schools will not work.

The case for changing by starting-new

Clayton Christensen, a professor at Harvard Business School, published *The Innovator's Dilemma* in 1997. The book seems mistitled: The dilemma exists really for the established operation, watching a disruptive innovation threaten its business and finding itself unable to respond. Happily he clarified this in an article in the March/April 2000 Harvard Business Review, "Meeting the Challenge of Disruptive Change", with Michael Overdorf. Their explanation illuminates the states' challenge in trying to make K-12 a self-improving institution.

Managers in successful corporations experiencing normal competition become quite skilled at responding with incremental changes and improvements, they wrote. The 'excellence' movement is full of examples. But occasionally—increasingly, it seems—private sector managers are confronted with "major disruptive change" that challenges existing practices in fundamental ways. And the existing organization is unable to adapt. Sometimes it is particular firms with particular products that are disrupted, sometimes whole industries.

The only way for an organization to respond successfully, Christensen found, is to acquire or to create a 'new organizational space' outside the old culture, values and processes. "When disruptive change appears managers . . . actually need to run two businesses in tandem, one whose processes are tuned to the existing business model and another that is geared toward the new model."

Their example from retailing rang a bell with Minnesotans. The five Dayton brothers had taken over the family's large and successful, high-class department store in downtown Minneapolis in the 1950s. They saw the region growing beyond the old city. They responded by opening department stores in the suburbs. Then at a convention about 1958 they heard a discussion about 'discounting'. Talking about this afterward they found discounting unattractive in some respects. But attractive as well: "Islands of loss in a sea of profit", Donald Dayton described it at the time. So in 1960 they went into discounting—by creating a wholly-owned subsidiary, Target Stores. Douglas Dayton became its CEO. Two stores opened in 1962. They were immediately successful. Quickly the department store group was complaining about Target cutting into its business. "But I didn't report to Ken" (his brother, who headed Stores), Doug Dayton says. "I reported to Bruce as chair of the corporate board".[1] Of all the department-store groups in America, Christensen says, only Dayton-Hudson made the transition successfully into discount retailing.

Some of those working in Minnesota on the problems of public education arranged for Christensen to present his analysis and conclusions to a national meeting on education policy. His presentation is worth quoting in full.

■ ■ ■ ■

I should start with where the puzzle came from.

---

[1]Conversation with Douglas Dayton, December 20, 2000.

I was living in Boston, watching Digital Equipment collapse. This had been a successful company. As in most such cases the success had been attributed to the management team. Now when it was failing the failure also was attributed to (bad) management. This was a common view. Yet it seemed strange. Clearly at the same time all the minicomputer firms were failing. And I had worked with DEC executives when I was with my own company. They were very good. I began to try to refine the problem. Is there really something about the style of management that causes good firms to fail?

I began looking at the disk-drive industry. I saw that no firm ever stayed 'on top' over a period of time, through successive generations of product. This began to generate a theory, which I then applied to other industries. It turned out to apply in other fields, including the non-profits, as well.

In every field there is a level of improvement the customers find useful (though of course the customers differ). There is also a level of performance-improvement in the product (or service) that the mainstream customers do not find useful; that is not what they need, so is not of interest. Firms do not necessarily get lazy as they grow. There are continuing, sustaining improvements. We found that 111 of the 116 identifiable improvements in disk drives were in this trajectory of 'sustaining' product-improvement. But five of the technological improvements that appeared during that period brought to market something that was, as we came to say, 'disruptive'. These were simple developments; not complex. But not things the mainline customers could use.

Let me go back to Digital. It was doing a wonderful job of sustaining improvement. At that time personal computers were toys. Apple was originally marketed to children. None of DEC's customers could use this, wanted this. The innovation took root in an undemanding market. And then the PC began improving, so rapidly that suddenly it *could* meet the needs of users who had previously been buying larger equipment.

Intel has thought about this. Low-end chips when they appeared took that company's market-share from 90% to 30% in 18 months. As Andy Grove said in one of our discussions: "It was a trivial technology that disrupted our company's business model". DEC faced this question. It had some proposals to go upscale in the minicomputer market, promising returns of 60%. It had some other proposals to move downscale to products that were lower in quality and which existing customers did not visibly want. It is virtually impossible for management to choose the latter. Yet almost every company whose stock today you wish you'd owned began as a company coming in at the low end of a market, making a product that the management of existing firms chose not to make.

■ This was the story of the telephone. Bell took his invention to Western Union, which asked: *"Three miles* is all the signal can carry?" and rejected his offer to sell the patents. In time the Forbes family put up the money for what became the Bell System. Telephony began not in the long-distance market but as a way of carrying voice signals between two offices of a single company. Over time research made it possible to extend the signal beyond three miles. In time the telephone blew Western Union out of the message market.

■ Consider Cisco. At the start packet-switching technology was no good for voice transmission. So the company started carrying data. The market for data grew and in time the technology for carrying voice-transmission improved. Cisco grew enormously.

■ Consider discount retailing. My father had a retail store. K-Mart came to town. It had a fundamentally different business model: With practically no help on the floor it was limited to selling goods the customers knew about, could simply come in and pick up . . . were able to buy without help. This initially took out the market for a lot of appliances, etc. Department stores then moved upscale to clothing, home furnishings. Gradually these stores were pushed to the high end of the market, continually pursued by the discount houses also continually upscaling.

■ Consider defense. At one point Secretary Cohen called and asked me to meet with the Joint Chiefs. They were interested because all their weapons systems had become oriented to massive, complex conflict with the Soviet Union. Suddenly that conflict had gone away, replaced by local wars and terrorism. The services were faced with a huge problem of reorienting to deal with this new kind of low-end problem.

As the conclusions emerged out of the research I wrote an article for the Harvard Business Review, which was initially rejected by the editor as "too pessimistic". The attitude was: You are saying that people build great firms and yet lose. The editor wanted solutions: Tell people what they can do to avoid losing. So we thought about all this some more. And we did find a few firms that had survived; had made the transition after being challenged by disruptive changes in their business. We saw that in all cases these had formed some kind of separate organization to work with the new technology even if it involved attacking the parent. We came to feel we could say with confidence there is zero probability that an organization can succeed against a disruptive technology by trying to handle the response from within its established operation.

Again, some examples will help.

- IBM is the only computer company to succeed through major changes in the product-cycle. When the minicomputer appeared to challenge the main-frames it set up a new operation in Rochester, Minn., to develop its System 360. When the personal computer appeared to challenge the mini it set up that skunk works in Florida, way away from IBM headquarters.

- Hewlett-Packard. When the ink-jet printer appeared HP was making big margins on its laser printers. Its printer division, located in Idaho, sat on the new technology. Finally management created a new division based in Vancouver WA to develop the new technology. The conflict between the two was horrendous. But it established HP in the market for the ink-jet printer as well.

- Dayton-Hudson. Of 300 department store companies only this one picked up successfully the disruptive technology of discounting. It created a wholly-owned subsidiary to build this business; given a new name—Target—to distinguish it from the company's top-line department stores. Target grew to become the dominant part of the business. Today the whole corporation has taken the name Target.

There is a theory behind all this.

Think of an organization as having (a) resources – people, cash, etc., (b) processes and (c) values. The processes include the patterns of operation; hiring, for example. They are built to serve the company's needs; are therefore not flexible . . . are intended not to change. So as they enable the company to do what it does they also make it unable to do something different. They determine what the company can not do. I use the term 'values' not to mean 'ethics' but more broadly, to mean the criteria by which people in the organization make decisions about what is important and what is not. Decisions of this sort are made in a great many individual situations within the organization. In a well-run organization the set of values is imposed on everyone, so everyone will be doing the things the organization has learned it needs to do to succeed.

As the firm grows managers cannot be interested in small opportunities promising low returns. So they lose the ability to innovate. A single organization will not give equal priority to two different kinds of operation. Values are very inflexible. They are meant not to change. This is, fundamentally, why the companies that succeeded against disruptive technologies had to set up new organizations. It was not a question of resources: The existing operation had the resources. It was a question of getting away from the existing processes and values.

Intel, again. As low-end computers grow, will it be able to change? Even with resources it was not clear it would be able to change. There were so many interdependencies with existing operations, and so many people involved that it was simply not possible to change quickly; for the existing operation to be successful at the low end of the chip business. So the decision was to set up a different organization, in Israel: Celeron. This, with a different mission and a different cost-structure made Intel a success.

Interestingly the problem is almost never that the organization cannot see the disruption coming at it. Many in fact see it and try to use it, simply failing. The firms making vacuum tubes all knew about the transistor; all tried to make it good enough to work in the products then using tubes. None of this worked. In fact the transistor first began to be used in hearing aids. Then in 1955 Sony came out with a crummy little portable radio; serving mainly the needs of teenagers. For a while this had no impact on the businesses using vacuum tubes. But in 1959 Sony brought out a portable television based on the transistor. This market became huge. This set could do everything the vacuum-tube products could do, and quickly it destroyed the firms with products based on vacuum tubes.[2]

The states must get beyond 'reform'

The governor and the legislature are top management for the state's public-education enterprise. In much the way the top management of Dayton-Hudson responded to the appearance of discounting by creating a new operation of its own, state policy leadership is now responding to the national demand for better education by opening a new 'subsidiary' outside its existing districts.

This was essential because the districts had been responding only incrementally to major disruptive changes.

Suburbs had appeared. Families moved out of the city, to new houses; other families moving into the old houses. In the process student populations changed dramatically. In the 1960s the courts ordered desegregation, accelerating the process. A very different youth culture emerged. In the mid-1970s enrollments crashed as the children of the baby boom graduated. The proportion of families with kids in school dropped sharply. Teachers unionized, to bargain collectively. Then came the computer, the Internet, the World Wide Web.

We sometimes forget how dramatically parents' educational levels have changed. In 1950 in Minnesota the median years of school completed by persons

---

[2]Author's notes of the interactive audio/video session with Christensen, at Hamline University in Saint Paul October 9-10, 2001, reprinted with permission.

over 25 was 8.5. Even by 1980 that had risen to about 14. I once asked an official of the Minnesota Education Association how the K-12 institution was different as a result of that shift, from most adults not having been to high school to most adults having some college. "I've never thought about that," he said.

Guaranteed their success and supported by tax revenues, the districts did not make dramatic adjustments to respond to these radical changes in their communities, their students, their political situation and the new technologies.[3] The different kids did not cause districts radically to change school: Kids who did not fit were moved out to alternative schools. There might be a challenge from computers at home but everybody agreed: 'It will never replace the real teacher'. Home school was a concern but people said: 'It will never grow large; kids need socialization'. The state might let somebody else start and run schools but these were dismissed as not really significant: too few, not high enough quality, not something we want to do.

Today, when the district sector is slow to respond to the introduction of the accountability model and the withdrawal of its exclusive, Christensen's conclusion about the need for the wholly-owned subsidiary cannot be dismissed. The cliché about the public sector being different than the private does not apply. His analysis does not hold up good private sector practice for the public sector to copy. Quite the reverse. It says that even with the authority of their management and the pressure of economic incentives private organizations do not and cannot change existing operations in fundamental ways. To say, "The public sector is different" would assert that political organizations are more flexible and better able to change. Who is going to assert that?

So the state needs to act. The state does not start or run schools, however, and is not itself likely to create schools. So the immediate question is how the state can create 'other entities' to oversee the creation of new schools.

How to create 'new organizational space'

Currently the states are creating the new organizational space mainly through the chartering laws. That is not the only possible way: The states might have created— could still create—a public corporation that would itself start and run schools. But with the exception of an occasional state arts or math/science school, states have not done that. Rather, their chartering laws create a new space in which various

---

[3]This is a classic case of what Albert Hirschman saw in the case of the Nigerian railways: public agencies made insensitive to change and the loss of patronage by their ability to draw on financing other than revenue from sales to customers. Hirschman himself drew the parallel with American schools, where attendance is mandatory and revenues are appropriated. See *Exit, Voice and Loyalty, Responses to Decline in Firms, Organizations and States*, Harvard University Press, 1970, pages 44-46.

sponsors authorize and oversee a variety of individuals and organizations starting schools. In effect the states charter sponsors; the sponsors then charter schools.

It is useful, as we saw in Chapter 7, to think of states creating this open sector at two levels. Partly within the district sector, by giving local boards authority to approve proposals for new schools outside the district administration. Partly outside the district sector, by letting new schools be authorized by other, non-district, entities. More and more states probably will arrange both kinds of new space. A state is likely to find its districts limited in their willingness to approve new schools that would challenge their existing schools. But the state owes its districts the chance to act if they will.

The state can build the new open sector outside the districts by enlarging the list of alternate sponsors designated or created by the chartering laws. There are two ways a state can act.

■ *States can add more existing entities as 'sponsors'*
By 2004, about half of the 41 chartering laws had authorized entities other than districts to sponsor new schools. Over time the list of available alternate sponsors has also become more varied: state boards of education have been added in some states, along with post-secondary institutions, municipal governments and large nonprofits. In recent years Minnesota (which began with local boards of education only) has had the most extensive list of entities designated by law to authorize new public schools. Any state can amend its law to add to its current list.

While adding sponsors the states can also make sponsoring more purposeful.

Up to now, everywhere, the role of the sponsor (school-authorizer) has been reactive. The original idea was that some community group or group of teachers would propose a school; the sponsor would then say 'Yes' or 'No'. Experience shows this has limitations. There is no obligation on the proposers to design schools that address the educational needs of the children of the community, or to use school models proven effective elsewhere. They may propose whatever kind of school they want. Discussion and decision occur on the proposals presented. Limited to approving or disapproving, the sponsor is likely to be only marginally involved in, committed to, what emerges.

A sponsor might instead be proactive. It might develop a sense of its own both about the learning needs and about the good learning models available. A sponsor might solicit designs from a variety of organizations, from among which it would choose. This would make chartering more a competitive process of selecting the best, less a process of saying 'Yes' or 'No' to proposals one at a time. Or a sponsor might actually select the learning design it likes and solicit proposals to set up and run schools using that design. In this expanded role the sponsor is likely to be more involved in what emerges.

There is a big plus in using alternate sponsors. Not being districts they do not run K-12 schools, so do not face the internal psychological and political constraints that complicate sponsorship for districts. They are often more open to creating different kinds of schools and to giving the school the autonomy it needs.

Offsetting this: Most alternate sponsors available at the moment have some other and much larger thing to do: run a university, operate a state department of education, carry on a large social-service program, manage a city. Universities with teacher-training programs might find chartering helpful to the main mission, to generate a 'lab' and professional-development school for the college of education. But for most non-district sponsors chartering is a distraction from the main mission, a burden. An alternate sponsor might charter a few schools. Few will charter many.

■ States can create new entities just to sponsor schools

There is a way for the state to get around this constraint. In generating alternate sponsors states are not limited to existing entities. They can create new entities, single-purpose sponsors whose only job is to authorize and oversee new public schools.

Two legislatures—Arizona's, and Congress acting for the District of Columbia—had created new boards of education authorized to approve new schools on the charter model. In 2004 a single-purpose sponsor was enacted in Colorado, Utah and Idaho and the idea was live again in South Carolina and Minnesota.

New entities of this sort somewhat resemble the orders found in the Catholic Church. This example from religion is not exact (and, please understand, implies nothing about vouchers). But the parallel, explained by the late James P. Shannon, former auxiliary bishop of the Archdiocese of Saint Paul and Minneapolis, is instructive.

The church has a hierarchy: The world is divided territorially into archdioceses and dioceses and parishes, presided over by the Pope and officials the Vatican appoints. But going back centuries the Church also created the Franciscans and the Cistercians and the Benedictines and in time the Jesuits and in recent years Mother Teresa's Missionaries of Charity. These orders are in a sense chartered. They can do anything the hierarchy can do: preach the gospel, heal the sick, teach the children; create churches, create hospitals, create schools. In Minnesota the University of St. Thomas belongs to the archdiocese, St. John's University belongs to the Benedictine order. The orders are outside the geographic boundaries of the hierarchy. They can set up anywhere.

Public education has a hierarchy. Public education has had no orders. The states can create orders, able to create schools outside the K-12 hierarchy. For that matter, so probably could the national government as well.

This open sector is in fact emerging

This is essentially what the states are now doing. Both the in-district and outside-the-district open sectors are appearing.

Since the Minnesota Legislature first acted in 1991 about 25 other state legislatures have enacted 'live' chartering laws that actually produce schools.[4] Against considerable odds, schools have been started. By 2004 something like 3,000 schools had appeared. In most of the major states the chartering law generated a wholly unexpected level of effort by parents, teachers and community organizations. It was a bumblebee: Both common sense and expert opinion tell us it cannot possibly fly but —unconcerned with what others think—the bumblebee flies anyway.

The charter sector is not an organization, not a project, not centrally directed and financed, not master-planned. Think of it as organic: more like the Internet than like a corporation; a piece of open architecture with nobody in overall control. Almost immediately it began to evolve, growing in size, continually showing us new variations in the laws and in the schools.

Some of the changes required going back to the legislature for approval: to raise or remove the cap on the number of schools allowed, to add other eligible sponsors, to adjust the mechanisms for oversight, to change or improve the financing arrangements, as for facilities. Some of it was simply the schools beginning to evolve new learning models, new practices, new forms of governance or, as Chapter 9 will explain, new arrangements for teachers. 'Evolving' seems quite the right word to use to describe the self-improving character of this new sector.

Among the new schools some important innovations are visible. Some are new models for learning. Some are new models of governance and management. Most early studies—as by the U.S. Department of Education—have not picked up this element of innovation.[5] As John Witte of the University of Wisconsin has pointed out, research tends to generalize; looks for central tendencies; looks to find 'most' and 'usually' and 'on the whole' and so looks less for the exceptional case that might

---

[4]The idea appeared spontaneously in different places about 1988-91. Joe Loftus, who works mainly in child welfare in Illinois, had the essential idea clearly thought out for Chicago in early 1989—only to have it rejected by those certain the answer was parent-run schools. In Britain the 'opt-out' program was part of the 1988 Education Act.

[5]Its 'Mapping' study, sampling schools in the charter sector, found significant differences from the default school in the district sector. Unfortunately this study got lost in 2001 in the transition between administrations and was never published.

be the breakthrough. Generalizations are misleading: The day after the Wright brothers' success at Kitty Hawk it would still have been possible to say that research and experimentation showed that 'most' heavier-than-air craft could not fly. What difference did the 'most' make, once Wilbur and Orville got it right?

More is appearing than just the schools. Focusing as it does on schools, the national discussion misses much about the infrastructure of the new sector. Chartering is organized mainly by state, the laws being state laws. In most chartering states the school operators have formed small trade associations. Friends' groups and resource centers have appeared, both to help with the start-up of schools and to work for improvements in the law.

By 1995 the state-level activity was beginning to be linked nationally, through a variety of organizations. Jon Schroeder in Saint Paul directed the Charter Friends National Network, a project of the Minnesota-based Center for Policy Studies in partnership with Hamline University. This advised on common problems (such as facilities, special education and contracting), followed federal legislation and brokered information—such as openings for personnel. In 2004 this was replaced by the (Washington-based) Charter School Leadership Council, chaired by Howard Fuller, long the key force of the reform coalition in Milwaukee. It will pull together the elements of, and be a voice for, 'the charter movement'. A National Association of Charter School Authorizers now pulls together the larger sponsors. The Center for Education Reform **www.edreform.com** in Washington, D.C., continues to track the sector closely, publishes the complete directory of chartered schools and keeps current a summary and analysis of the charter laws. The regional lab in San Francisco, WestEd, issues a helpful email newsletter, on contract to the U.S. Department of Education. The department has run the recent annual national gatherings-of-the-clan and administers a growing program of start-up aid distributed through the states. Several large foundations provide venture capital for the design and start-up of new and new-model schools and increasingly to support the evolving infrastructure. So-called 'education management organizations' that sell curriculum or management to schools in the charter sector are organizing, as are groups that help in financing facilities.

How do we tell if 'new schools' is working?

As this new sector appears within public education people naturally ask, "Is it working?" Unfortunately, people tend to see what's happening mainly as 'charter schools'—which leaves it unclear whether the question is asking about the schools or about the states' new strategy for improvement.

To answer the question we will need a new set of concepts and a change in the way we think and talk. But it isn't really so hard.

The first step is to get the language right. People visibly struggle for some term to distinguish the institutional change from the schools created, often failing and using the same term—'charter schools'—to refer to both these quite different things. It is best not to talk of 'charter schools'. When we mean the schools we should say chartered schools. When we mean the system change we should say chartering.

Chartered schools do differ from district-owned schools. This new sector is organized on principles different from those in the district sector. Its schools have boards, removed from electoral politics. The schools have authority to decide how to teach. They select their own personnel and handle their own finances. They are to be accountable for performance, not just for compliance. This autonomy is important, gives them an opportunity to be different. Chartering is, as Allan Odden at the University of Wisconsin says, America's principal experiment with school-based decision-making.

But the chartered school is not a kind of school in any pedagogical sense. A charter is best thought of as a license to start a school. It is an empty institutional structure, as a building is an empty physical structure. What matters is what you put into it. And people do put very different kinds of programs into the schools they create. Christine Jax, when commissioner in Minnesota, used to say: "If you've seen one charter school you've seen . . . one charter school".

Some schools are small, some are not small. Some use a proven model, some try a new model. Some are high-tech, some low-tech. Some have teachers talking to kids in groups, some use project-based learning. In some kids dress as they please, in others they wear uniforms. Some organize on the bureau model used in districts, some on the contract model. Some have principals, some are run by their teachers in a partnership. Some are free-standing organizations, some belong to a centrally-managed group. Some are sponsored by districts, some are not sponsored by districts. Some are non-profit, some are commercial. Some are created new, some are conversions. On and on.

Studies that try to generalize about 'charter schools' are almost always inconclusive, almost always report that the evidence is mixed—as of course it would be.

Evaluation needs to disaggregate. It is important to know that computers are different than typewriters. But that is not quite enough, is it? We probably want to know how a given computer differs from others, so we can decide which is best for us. Similarly, we want to know: In schools of what sort do students (of what sort) do better? In schools of what sort do they do less well? Evaluation should tell us which differences make what difference. Researchers who try to generalize about 'charter schools' miss much of what it is important to see.

This perspective will help us focus on evaluating chartering as an institutional innovation, as a strategy for change and improvement.

■ *Is chartering replicating good models and good practice?*

Chartering is a way to create new schools that are more than incrementally different from those in the community today. But different does not have to mean 'innovative'. Not every new school needs to be a model never tried before.

A new school can be created to replicate a proven model of school. This may be done to bring into the community a model not now present. Or to expand a model for which demand is growing. This is happening, as people use the new sector to set up KIPP schools, Core Knowledge schools, Success For All schools. We need to know how far the chartering program is in fact replicating quality learning models.

■ *Is chartering generating new models and new practices?*

A charter does, however, offer an opportunity to try some truly different things. So some new schools are likely to be innovative. This means chartering is in part a research-and-development program, discovering new models for learning, for governance and for management.

Albert Shanker used the image of discovery to explain his charter proposal to the National Press Club in March 1988.[6] There, and later in his columns in the Sunday *New York Times,* he talked about Henry Hudson being 'chartered' by The Crown: Go out and find something important and come back and tell Us about it. Not every captain discovered something; not every ship came back. But Henry Hudson discovered the bay that now bears his name and brought back word of the harbor that became New York.

Trying things and evaluating results, doing more of what seems to work, phasing-out what seems not to work, is the way most things improve. The scale of the trials should be kept small so that errors will be small and can be quickly corrected. This greater opportunity to try things distinguishes the open sector from the district sector and will help make K-12 a self-improving institution.

■ *Are the chartered schools succeeding?*

Ultimately chartering must produce good schools. So evaluation will need to ask: How many of the schools are good schools? And ask again: What is a 'good' school?

New and different kinds of schools will require new kinds of assessment. It will be important to look with fresh eyes for what is working well in these schools. It may not be high scores. It may be gain on scores. Or it may be better attitudes, better attendance, more student initiative, greater curiosity about learning. Academics are important but not all-important. Safety is important. A healthy school culture is

---

[6]Apparently picking up the term from Ray Budde, an educator in New England.

important. Empowerment is important. The public wants many things from its schools.

Everyone will need to understand that in their early years the new start-ups will almost always look lower in quality. The chartered schools usually get less money than schools in the district sector. So they are unlikely to match district schools in the experience of their faculty or in the quality of their facilities or the breadth of their extracurricular programs. New schools need some time. It takes a while to get any new operation working well. In the meantime, and especially where the students enrolling come poorly prepared and performing below grade level, these schools will not look good when evaluated against established schools using conventional measures and conventional expectations.

The concept of success is not simple. A school may be failing on one dimension but succeeding on others. So we will need multiple measures. It will help, too, to listen to the people in the school; to teachers and to students and their parents. Where people appear to be highly satisfied with their schools, evaluators need to inquire why. "The degree to which we shy away from (satisfaction) in judging the quality of schools, especially in research, is extraordinary", John Goodlad has written. In most areas judgments about satisfaction are the measure of success.

■ *Is chartering a superior strategy for improvement?*

Even if some of the schools fail, the strategy that includes a major effort to start new schools should move improvement faster than a strategy limited to trying to transform existing schools. This question of strategy itself needs evaluation. In early 2004 the national government's new Institute of Educational Studies was soliciting proposals to create a center for evaluating strategies. And the Bill & Melinda Gates Foundation was a couple of years along with an evaluation of its effort to get small, student-focused, technology-intensive secondary schools—partly by creating these schools new and partly by trying to break down existing high schools. Early results found new schools the more productive strategy.[7]

A related question will be whether—as the new open sector grows—the districts will work harder to change and improve their existing schools. This is a tricky question, as we have seen. Chartered schools cannot change district schools: Only districts can change district schools. Still, the appearance of schools run by others, attracting students and dollars, is bound to create a new reason for the district to make changes it might not have made in its schools otherwise. Evaluation should ask which boards and superintendents do decide to respond, and which do not, and why.

-----

[7]See www.smallhs.sri.com.

Evaluation must factor-in the character of chartering as a trial and error process. No sensible business would evaluate its R&D program by the no-defects standard it sets for the proven models it uses in its production processes. Some experiments will not work well in their early years. Some will not work at all. But a failed experiment does not mean a failed program. Chartering can be succeeding even though not all the schools chartered are succeeding.

Chartering will need to be evaluated over time. Most things improve, evolve. The schools will; the laws and state policies will.

Finally, evaluation should be diagnostic, as testing should be diagnostic. It should tell us what is going well and what is not, and what to adjust and how, advising states what they should do to make the program work better.[8]

Where do the teachers come in?

In talking about creating schools and about making schools different it's easy to slide over the question about who does the designing, planning and proposing; easy to slide by the role of teachers. Most discussions about policy, about re-forming the institution and even about improving learning do not think mainly about teachers as the major actors.

It is time now to think about the role of teachers. This might just be the greatest area of unrealized and untapped potential.

---

[8] A full explanation of the challenge of evaluating chartering can be found on **www.EducationEvolving.org**, along with a "model request-for-proposals" for a state's evaluation both of its chartering strategy and of the schools chartered.

■ ■ ■ ■ ■ ■
Chapter **9**

LET THE TEACHERS LEAD
THE LEARNING, IF THEY WISH

The discussion about teaching and learning is mired in old conceptions about what teachers do and about what teachers are.

Teaching has been largely instruction; the technology of an adult talking, a group of students listening and responding to questions.[1] The key questions about teaching and teachers—about teacher training, teacher practice, teacher recruitment and retention, teacher compensation—are all discussed within this framework. Minds are locked into the old assumption that if you want to be a teacher you have to be an employee.

The assumption of employment makes the effort at improvement a program of professional development organized by management. This is assumed to be the most effective way to secure the changes in teaching practice that researchers and policymakers are convinced are now required. Improving teaching is not something teachers do in their own interest. It is, clearly if implicitly, something the boss does.[2]

The assumption of employment does not encourage the notion of teachers either as professionals or as leaders: The administrators are the leaders.[3] Teachers may want to think of teaching as a profession. But teachers do not control the way the work is done, which is the test of being a professional. Most similar occupations offer their people the option to work as professionals, solo or with partners in single- or multi-specialty groups. Not education. In education the rule is almost absolute:

---

[1]See page 33.

[2]Or tries to do. A few years back Minneapolis scheduled some professional-development days to improve the teaching of reading. Not a lot of teachers attended. So the district rescheduled the sessions. By then it had used all the days allowed by the contract for professional development. So it offered to pay teachers to attend. Nope: Can't do that, the union said; not even if you pay. The district protested: We did schedule the days and teachers were supposed to come. They just didn't. To which the union replied: That's a management problem you have to deal with.

[3]Though Minnesota Statutes 122A.42 still says, "The teacher shall have the general control and government of the school".

If you want to be a teacher you have to be an employee. The old provision survives as an anachronism. In reality teachers do not control the professional life of the school. I remember a meeting where a senior person with (then) Group Health was explaining its two boards: the corporate board for business affairs and the medical/dental board for the professional issues of its—mostly employed—physicians. The teachers saw immediately: Our district has only a corporate board. Where's our 'medical/dental board'?

Within the school building the principal is the instructional leader more in theory than in reality. 'Principal' was once an adjective: principal teacher. Today 'principal' has become a noun; is an administrator. But the old notion of instructional leader hangs on largely because boards appoint principals and guard jealously as a management right their authority to control professional issues.

These old notions need to be re-thought. If the object is to improve teaching we should be looking for an arrangement that mobilizes teachers' energies and abilities fully toward change and improvement, that gives teachers a real opportunity to improve what they do and reasons to make these changes in their own interest. This is essential to make education a self-improving institution.

Happily, teachers could work for themselves in the way most professionals have long been able to do. By 2003 this arrangement had emerged and was developing in the charter sector both in Minnesota and in Wisconsin, in districts as different as Henderson, Minn., (pop. 910) and Milwaukee, with results and implications worth thinking about.

The New Country School
An hour southwest of the Twin Cities area on U.S. 169 as you turn west on state highway 19, drop down the bank of the Minnesota River valley and cross the bridge you are in Henderson. Just to the right on Main Street is a tan metal building that blends with the lovely warm brick in which most of the old river town is built. The building houses the Minnesota New Country School.

You may have seen this school in USA Today or on network television. It was students from New Country who found the deformed frogs. Their discovery of the frogs with extra legs and missing legs quickly became a matter of serious interest within the adult scientific community, and became of course an exceptional learning opportunity for the students.[4]

The school was formed in 1993 largely by teachers from LeSueur High School, dissatisfied with the old model of—as one of them said—"kids coming to school to watch teachers work". These teachers wanted students to feel responsible for their own learning. There was no way they could persuade the board to

---

[4]The students' discovery opens William Souder's A *Plague of Frogs*, Hyperion Press, 2000.

change the district high school. It was Minnesota's chartering law that gave them the opportunity to put their idea into practice by creating a different school new.

Teachers and administrators at the high school resisted the proposed new school. They did not criticize the learning design. They said a new school would take students and money away from the high school. The superintendent, Harold Larson, and the board chair, Virginia Miller, supported the proposal. At the decisive board meeting she said: It's not our money. It's the students' money, the state's money. The charter was approved. The school opened in September 1994 in some old storefronts on Main Street in LeSueur.

Walk today into the new building through the south door and to your left is a small media room with books and videotapes. Then a small lunchroom. Beyond are rooms for art and 'shop'. To your right and behind you there is a science lab and a greenhouse. Most of the building is a large open room; a high central area and a one-story area beyond on two sides. There is a small administrative area in the near corner. On the south side of the central area is a bright blue metal silo with one side cut out to form a stage.

It does not look like a school. There are no corridors, no oak doors with little slit windows through which you see a teacher facing a class, talking. Most students are at work-stations, singly or in pairs. Teachers are at their desks or with a student at a work-station. It looks much like a newspaper city room or, as a consultant once said, like "a messy Kinko's". The place is orderly but not still and not quiet. Most people are seated but some are moving around. There is a hum of conversations.

This is a secondary school. It has about 120 students. In regular school they would be in grades 7–12. New Country, though, is basically ungraded. Kids of different ages work together. Each has an adviser. Each adviser has about 17 students. Students choose their adviser and remain with the adviser they choose through their years in the school. MNCS was never formally in Ted Sizer's Coalition of Essential Schools but its program takes a lot from his notion of student as worker, teacher as coach. When it dedicated its new building in the spring of 1998 the school brought Ted and Nancy Sizer to Henderson as the the principal guests.

The students are pretty much a cross-section of rural Minnesota. Some of their parents farm. Some work in town. A few are professors or other professionals in nearby college towns. Almost 20 percent of the students are now special-education students, but it is hard to identify most of these since in this school everybody is on an individual learning plan. On any given day some students are not at the school: They are in the community working on a project or in a course at Gustavus Adolphus College or Mankato State University.

Several features of this school are worth some discussion.

■ *The reduction in scale*

The size of this school is striking.

Not long ago the notion was that a good high school had to be a big school. Much influential opinion held that a broad list of courses defined the good high school. The plan for rebuilding Minneapolis' high schools in 1963, for example, said it was "generally accepted" that a high school should have a minimum 1,000 students. Only a big school could afford the teacher-specialties required. Through the whole period after 1950 high schools kept getting larger. A few voices were raised in protest, some like Thomas Wilson in *High Schools as Communities* arguing that "schools should be of a size such that every student is needed". But until quite recently these voices went largely unheeded.

This has begun to change. It is clearer now that the decisions that produced schools with 700, 800 or 1,000 kids in a graduating class were not decisions primarily in the interest of students. Carlos Medina, with the Center for Educational Innovation in New York City, went to a high school with 6,000 students. He says simply: "Small schools are more important than small classes".

In June 1991 at the meeting of the Minnesota Association of School Business Officials, there was a brief presentation about the state's newly-enacted charter law. Afterward Joel Sutter came up to the speaker to comment about the new law. Sutter had left the staff of the Minnesota Senate to become the business officer for Rosemount/Apple Valley, a large suburban district on the south side of the Twin Cities area. "That's a good idea," he said. "We're now bringing Eagan High school up to 2,000 students. After that we'll build another 2,500-student school, and probably another one after that. We should not be doing this: It's both bad education and bad economics. It's wrong to be offering all kids only high school with 800 students in the graduating class." And given the demographics of new-suburban development, he said, "We'll be closing those buildings before they're paid for".

Below a certain size the course-and-class model is hard to sustain: a biology teacher and a chemistry teacher and a physics teacher, teachers specializing in Spanish and French, someone for social studies, and all the teachers of English and math. New Country has solved this problem by dispensing with courses and classes and moving to project-based learning technology that relies partly on computers and the web.

The conventional thinking about the need for large schools may be wrong. The experience at New Country shows it is possible to maintain economically and educationally viable secondary schools at very small scale; in very small communities and, if we wish, within cities as well. Its new model has huge implications, is extraordinarily important, especially for rural America where enrollments are in decline.

■ *The learning model: No courses and no classes*

Except for morning groupings in math the New Country School has no courses and no classes. In this school students spend the day working on their projects. Some are individual projects, some are group projects. Some involve activity within the building, some take the student out to work with others. Projects emerge from a discussion among the student, the adviser and the student's parents. The projects are designed to require the student to learn science and math and history and social science. The projects require them to improve their reading. The students write, to document their work. Periodically they present their projects to teachers and parents and community people. This requires them to learn to communicate orally. For some students the project may be a course at a nearby college through Minnesota's Post-secondary Options program.

I listened once to a person from the Education Commission of the States talking with a student about his project on creationism. The boy was curious about the controversy that was causing people to get elected and un-elected to the state board of education in Kansas. It's a question that opens in many directions. It's history: Darwin and the Voyage of the Beagle. It's natural science. It's genetics. It's religion and theology. It's drama: Read "Inherit the Wind" about the Scopes trial: Clarence Darrow and William Jennings Bryan. And it's politics. A good adviser and an enterprising student can open all these dimensions.

■ *The organizational model: No employees*

In addition to having no courses and no classes the school has no employees. After taking the initiative to form the school the teachers decided to organize as a workers' cooperative and to have the cooperative run the program on contract to the school.

New Country itself, like all chartered schools in Minnesota, is a nonprofit corporation. The corporation has a board. This board has only contracts: with the owner of the building for its space, with the district for some bus transportation and extracurriculars, with a caterer for lunch. For the learning program the board has a lump-sum contract with an entity called EdVisions, which is the teachers.

EdVisions is a Chapter 308A organization under Minnesota law, legally a co-operative, generically a small professional partnership. Through this partnership the teachers and others run the program of learning for the school and its administration.[5] They control the professional issues: design the program, select the learning methods and materials, manage the budget, recruit their colleagues, evaluate their performance, run a program for the improvement of practice and decide their own compensation.

---

[5]The partnership could, of course, employ administrators and support staff, so that only teachers would be partners and so teachers would only teach.

At the school the members divide up the work. There is little administration as such. One of the teachers handles the accounts and payroll, someone else serves as the lead teacher, another handles the hardware and software technology, another makes out the reports to the state. For the extra work they receive additional payment.

For the first four years they operated the school out of a collection of storefronts on Main Street in LeSueur, once the home of Green Giant brand peas and corn. In 1998 the school moved into the new building built for it six miles up the road in Henderson. The $1.3 million building was built for about $70 a square foot; about half the cost of new school buildings elsewhere in rural Minnesota.

In 1999 the co-operative began to grow. It added three small elementary schools converted by their districts to charter status. It won approval from the state for another new secondary school, in Mankato, which opened in September 2000. That fall it also contracted to operate a new secondary in south Minneapolis: El Colegio. It now also has Avalon and the High School for the Recording Arts, inner-city secondaries in Saint Paul. Other schools have since opened in Duluth, Hutchinson, Northfield and Bemidji.

In the spring of 2000 Tom Vander Ark visited the Henderson school. Vander Ark heads the education program for the Bill & Melinda Gates Foundation. Quickly he included EdVisions in the network of small, focused, technology-intensive secondary schools whose replication the foundation is supporting around the country. In January of 2001 EdVisions launched its project to create up to 15 more such schools in the Midwest over the next three years. Gates later made another investment to allow the model to expand nationally.

EdVisions itself has been almost continually evolving. At the start it was one cooperative for one school. By 2003 the cooperative had about 125 members in 10 or more schools, with the teachers at each school site making informally the kinds of decisions about professional issues that New Country made when it was EdVisions' only school. EdVisions itself now functions essentially as a service cooperative, handling mainly payroll and benefits. It is possible that teachers at individual sites will organize separate cooperatives as a vehicle for the professional decisions at their site. If so it would then resemble the arrangement emerging in Milwaukee.

Now teachers' cooperatives in Milwaukee

About 1997 a vanload of teachers from Milwaukee went to Henderson to spend a day in New Country. Driving home they decided they would like to create such a school in Milwaukee, and on the cooperative model. Two years later an age-four-kindergarten to grade-eight elementary, the I.D.E.A.L. school, appeared. By fall 2004 there were six teacher-cooperative schools operating.

Milwaukee is evolving a significant variation on the original model. In Minnesota teachers in chartered schools are included in the state teacher-retirement program. In Wisconsin they are not. So Cris Parr and her colleagues quickly discovered they would need to adapt the idea for their situation. She went to her father, who had spent his career in the labor movement, mostly with the big AFSCME local in the Milwaukee area. John Parr and a labor-lawyer friend quickly worked out a way for the teachers to leave their economic life with district employment, the master contract and union membership and to form the cooperative as a vehicle for their professional life.

Listen to Cris Parr explaining her school—her second co-op school, the Professional Learning Institute, a high school—to a forum convened by the Progressive Policy Institute in Washington, D.C., in November 2003:[6]

> Cris Parr: I'd been teaching 17 years in Milwaukee public schools. The district's graduation rates and scores were atrocious. I was frustrated with how little I could accomplish outside my classroom. I was in an IGE school ("individually guided education"). A new principal proposed changing it, dropping IGE. Parents and teachers didn't know what to do. A member of the MPS board, John Gardner, suggested we start our own school. We heard about New Country. We drove there, spent a day. We came back so excited. On the five-hour drive we started talking about how to adapt this model to MPS.

> I'd been active in the union. Under Wisconsin's charter law we would not have been able to stay in the retirement program, using the New Country model. We started up I.D.E.A.L. on a slightly different model. We were the first new MPS instrumentality charter. This was about the time Bill Andrekopoulos went from Fritsche middle school to be superintendent.

> I.D.E.A.L. is now in its third year. As the 8th-graders began leaving they went into high schools that were very traditional. The kids started asking for a different kind of high school. So after two years of planning we now have the Professional Learning Institute, P.L.I.

> In our arrangement all the teachers remain district employees, under the master contract and members of the union. We *select* our teachers. They are hired by the district. MPS is a very dynamic situation right now. With the grant from the Gates Foundation it's pushing to create 40 new schools. North Division high school, for example, where about 20 per cent of the kids graduate, now has four small schools in it. These gradually will replace the old North Division.

---

[6]To see the full text of the presentation by Cris Parr and Dee Thomas from Minnesota New Country School go to **www.EducationEvolving.org**.

We've had awesome support from our union. We generate no grievances against administrators; create no work. I keep the union posted on developments. I was the union rep in my building all the past 17 years.

I have almost the same list as Dee of the things that have changed for me.

- I got the keys to my building. It feels like my building now. I can see the same feeling in the kids. They scrounged up a lot of the furniture over the summer; cleaned it. They like the school. We often have to throw them out. "It's 7 p.m., time to go home."

- We have extra responsibility. I spent years not caring about the budget or where the toilet paper came from. Here I have to think about these things. And the kids are involved, too. We involve them in interviews: One student was the decisive vote on a clerical person, who has turned out to be just great.

- Charters in MPS are evaluated every five yers. I'm more accountable than in the traditional school. And I'm OK with this. MPS is now moving to value-added as a measure. This longitudinal performance is important. Our school has 98% attendance, every day. If a kid is absent I'm on the phone: We've gone to pick up kids. Accountability has got to be more than test scores.

- Some of our MPS schools are becoming multiplexes. We now have four schools in our building. These may join together to hire, say, a business manager to serve them all.

- We're the only school that has a student's voice answering our phone, and we catch some flak for doing that. Yesterday we sent six kids to the meeting of the MPS high-school task force, to get into the discussion with 150 adults. The kids are our best salesmen.

- We have a lot more flexibility along with the responsibility. This can be hard for people who'd gotten used to blaming others. Our biggest challenge is to adjust to this new situation.

- The momentum is growing. I see no way to stop this. It is exciting now, after so many years of having to take direction I often disagreed with. If it weren't for Gates all this might not be happening. But they invest in this small-school arrangement.

Most people do not have a picture in their head for this arrangement. They know teachers only as employees. They assume that in chartered schools the teachers would be employees of the school. So when the union sets out to organize a chartered school, for example, it thinks of forming a small bargaining unit at the school; re-creating the adversary relationship between employer and employees that exists at the district level. Others think this way as well.

In the Milwaukee arrangement the teachers form a cooperative, a partnership, at the school. The charter is in effect issued to them, to the cooperative. Through the cooperative the teachers make the professional decisions about the school. They are employees of the district, not of the school. Each teacher-position is paid according to the district salary scale, but the teachers can decide how many positions of which sort to have. And, as Cris Parr indicates, they can select and de-select teachers, returning any de-selected to the district's pool of employed teachers. As she notes, the union has been good about entering into memoranda of understanding that waive certain provisions of the master contract to permit these schools to operate as the teachers feel necessary. The teachers are, after all, the union's dues-paying and voting members. The school gets flexibility, the teachers control professional issues while remaining protected economically, and the union keeps its members and their dues.

Joe Graba, an attendee at meetings of the Teacher Union Reform Network, brought Cris and John Parr to its February 2003 meeting. They got a positive reception for their idea. But as one union local executive said to Graba afterward: We cannot lead this from the top. It will have to come from teachers who want to do it.

Would they like to? In a 2003 survey of teachers' attitudes Public Agenda asked one question (sort-of) about ownership: "How interested would you be in working in a charter(ed) school run and managed by teachers?" The response was stunning: 58% of teachers in the national sample said they would be somewhat or very interested in that arrangement; 65% of the new (less than five years) teachers and even 50% of the veteran (over 20 years) teachers.

What if we trusted teachers to decide?

With the autonomy provided by the charter law and with the authority themselves to make the decisions within the cooperative, these teachers are doing dramatically different things both with governance and with the learning methods in their schools. People who hear them talk about their experience are struck especially by the sense of motivation that has been created in the teachers and in the students.

It is just possible that the best way to address the challenges with teachers and teaching will be to expand the use of the professional-partnership arrangement.

The traditional arrangement is clearly full of problems

It does appear the effort to change and to improve teacher practice is running into heavy seas. The idea is for teachers to think less about 'my classroom' and more about 'my school'. There is an effort to develop the concept of 'professional communities' as a way to encourage teachers to think and act collegially. Yet, perhaps because the strategy gives so little attention to changing structure, there has been no thought of teachers actually forming a professional group. Teachers remain employees. Administrators organize 'professional development'—coaching, classes—for them. Perhaps not surprisingly, many teachers balk; "are not buying in" to the effort to 'improve instruction'. This is a serious problem for the effort at reform.

Existing arrangements are not well designed to motivate teachers to improve. The effort at improvement relied heavily—as Jack Frymier wrote in 1969 in *Fostering Educational Change*—on altruism as the motivational base for change. "We say in effect to the teachers involved, 'Here is a new idea. Try it out. Work hard. Learn all of the new factors and skills and knowledge involved. If you really try and really put yourself into it, children will learn more by the end of the year and you will feel good about it'."[7]

Also, the traditional arrangement limits teachers' career opportunities. For teachers who want to grow in income and in status the route is open into administration. But for a teacher committed to teaching there is little concept of being promoted.[8] At some point teachers realize that on the last day they work they may be doing essentially what they were doing on the first day they worked: standing in a room talking to 30 kids: 'Cell and bell', as the old expression has it.

In the summer of 1984 the principal consultant for the Minnesota Business Partnership, Paul Berman, convened a small meeting to test emerging findings and proposals. One of those present was Arlen Gunderman, then an elementary principal in the Mounds View district. An unusual principal, past president of the National Association of Elementary School Principals, his office was full of old farm implements and Teddy Bears. "Candidly," Gunderman said that day, "my job as a principal is to motivate, as much as I can and for as long as I can, people who are in essentially dead-end jobs."

There is an impulse in good teachers to feel professional; to feel they own their work. A former Minnesota Teacher of the Year said in a meeting about this: "I used to think I worked for myself"—though he added, "I guess I can't really say that any more". His comment catches the concern many teachers have about the impulse in much recent policy to reduce teachers' discretion, to get teachers to adopt and to follow what others decide is best practice. But also, of course, that impulse to think in terms of 'my classroom'.

The concern is that as employees the teachers may not respond either to

---

[7]Charles E. Merrill Publishing Co., 1969.

[8]Teachers rise in salary with seniority and with education that earns them a master's or doctor's degree. And, of course, as a result of their union's work to bargain-up the pay scale.

directives or to appeals to altruism, and may not develop the collegiality required to focus the school on the improvement of student learning.

The incentives in ownership carry real promise

The intriguing possibility, the hypothesis that comes out of the early work of these partnerships in Minnesota and Milwaukee, is that to increase the rate at which better practices come into school policymakers should give teachers collectively the incentives that come with ownership. When work and ownership are combined good practice and new technology tend to be taken up quickly. This might be a structural change that would pay off both in improved learning and in greater productivity.

Think about the simplified summary of the economy's evolution from farmer to (factory) worker to clerk:

■ On the family farm work and ownership were combined. Farmers made the investment decisions; farmers reaped the returns. After about 1870 American agriculture began to take up new equipment and new methods. Better plows, tractors and other farm machinery, better seeds, better cropping practices: All these spread rapidly in the Midwest and Great Plains. The improvements made the farmer's labor at once easier and more profitable. The technology of farming changed and productivity soared. The proportion of the population engaged in agriculture plummeted. There were fewer farmers, most significantly better off.

■ As the scale of enterprise enlarged in the industrial era, work and ownership separated. The workers became employees. When owners made investments the owners captured the rewards. The workers had to organize and fight to win a share of the productivity gains. Sometimes, where they could not share in the gains, the workers resisted the introduction of new machinery and new practices.

■ Now we're in the information era. It's fascinating to ask people: "Which of the two earlier eras is this information era inherently more like?" Usually people will say: like farming. Then ask: "Now tell me why we have education organized on the industrial model?

Clearly smaller scale lends itself to combining work and ownership. School— and teaching—can be organized at small scale: the program, the school, the department. It can also be organized collegially. It simply has not been, traditionally. "Little in the zeitgeist of American public education promotes teachers' sense of agency or collective responsibility", Milbrey McLaughlin and Joan Talbert write.[9] It could be. Certainly the capital costs of going into teaching are lower than the capital costs of going into farming.

---

[9] In *Professional Communities and the Work of High School Teaching*, University of Chicago Press, 2001.

Companies producing computer hardware and software may have been marketing to the wrong people. They have been marketing to districts; trying to persuade the boss to bring in the new equipment for the employees to use. It has not been an outstanding success. Sometimes equipment is bought but not really used. I remember talking to Bill Ridley one day in the 1980s about the idea of moving the decision to the teachers. He was then handling K-12 education for Control Data Corporation. He shook his head. "I haven't got time to talk to the teachers," he said.

That was rational, realistic. The education industry quite naturally takes the institution as it stands. Teachers do not now make the decisions about technology: The superintendent and the board control the budget and make those decisions. To suggest that before marketing its products the industry should first have persuaded policymakers to rearrange the institution, transferring the investment decision from management to the teachers, would have been regarded as very strange indeed. "Not practical", people would have said.

It is amazing how often people think it is not practical to do what is necessary. Sometimes, as in billiards, success requires playing a carom shot.

Choices for teachers

Teachers who get—who take—the opportunity to be collectively in charge of their work, to create the kind of learning program they believe will be effective, will not all create the kind of school we see in New Country and in Milwaukee. Some will create quite different and perhaps quite traditional schools.

The combination of chartering and partnership provides that choice for teachers. It is important for teachers to have, as David Ferrero of the Gates Foundation has pointed out so nicely, the opportunity to put into practice the philosophy they believe in—whether a progressive philosophy or a liberal-arts and basic-education philosophy—rather than to have to fight endlessly within the school and district about which is 'right'.[10]

Teachers will then have two decisions: what they want the school to be and whether they want to work as employees or as partners in a professional group. For the moment these options are available together, in chartered schools created new. With some changes in law or in the master agreement they could be available also in existing district schools. Were districts and their unions willing to make those changes the way would be open for a small professional group to run, say, the math department or science department or language department of a big suburban high school.

---

[10]See "Why Choice Is Good for Teachers: Ending the Pedagogical Holy Wars", *Education Next*, Winter 2004.

Teachers might run a school—or a department, or program

It is entirely conceivable that education could offer teachers the opportunity to work for themselves as engineers and architects and consultants and lawyers and physicians may if they wish. The assumption of employment is simply another of those features of K-12 explainable only on grounds that "This is the way it's always been".

The idea of teachers owning the program or a department was put one evening in the 1980s to a half-dozen math teachers in a big high school in the Rosemount/Apple Valley, Minn., district. Collectively you would have the budget for the department, you could decide how math would be taught, you would have to show that student learning improved but if you did you could keep either for use in the program or as personal income whatever you did not need to spend. The question was not, "Would you do this?". It was, "Assume this were the arrangement in your school. What would begin to happen?"

The teachers were quiet for a while. Then they began to list things they could do. We would get kids working independently, we would get kids helping other kids, we would get parents helping at the home end, we would get community people helping, if one of us moved away we would probably shuffle the duties and hire an aide, and we would certainly take a look at how computers might help.

What more are we looking for?

Objections quickly arise, all predictable, all commonly heard. Teachers should not be trying all the time to figure out something new, they should do what works. Teachers don't know anything about administration, they just want to be left alone to teach. Teachers will win professional status some day through bargaining. And so forth.

Perhaps these are valid reasons not to change. But perhaps not. Perhaps they're simply apologies for the status quo.

Ownership might unlock some doors

By aligning teachers' collective interest with the public interest in change and improvement the ownership/partnership idea offers the potential to solve some critical problems about how to change teaching and improve learning.

Late in 2000 a policy project sponsored by Hamline University in Saint Paul began an effort to think through more carefully the idea of teacher professional ownership: the what of it, the why of it, the how of it.

Headed by Edward J. Dirkswager, the steering committee was a mix of persons; some knowledgeable about K-12 and its issues, some professionals working in partnerships in law, medicine, accounting, auditing and consulting, some with long experience in the cooperative movement, some from EdVisions.

The idea received its first national discussion at a meeting at Hamline September 25–26, 2001. A book, *Teachers as Owners*, was finished in the summer of 2001, distributed at the Hamline meeting and published in June 2002 by Scarecrow Education Press.

Providing incentives for teachers—offering professional groups the opportunity to change schooling and reasons to do so in their own interest—might solve five important problems facing K-12 education.

1. *To get school to motivate students*

Traditional school with its courses and classes is not well tuned to the differences among students. High schools, especially, are large. The schools are age-graded: A student is with one teacher for a year; next year, with another. Students cannot spend more time on a topic they are slow to understand or that especially interests them. Much of what they are assigned they find uninteresting, not challenging. This is not a model calculated to motivate today's students.

The learning model used by the New Country School or Avalon School and by the project-based schools in Milwaukee emphasizes individual differences. The schools are small and kids stay with their adviser year after year. Students work on projects of interest to them; the work is self-paced. Not surprisingly there are few discipline problems.[11] "In my prior life as principal in a district high school my problem was to get kids to come to school", Dee Thomas said while lead teacher at New Country. "In this school my problem is to get them to go home."

It was not easy to get students to be responsible for their own learning. Both students and teachers had grown up in the old model of teacher as worker. But today if you walk around these schools, asking students about their work, you are struck by the seriousness with which they answer.

Students are also involved in the decision about who comes to teach at New Country. Dee Thomas tells about the day a candidate came to meet with the selection committee when she was lead teacher. Around the table were three adults and three students. As the discussion started Thomas said to the candidate: "Everyone around the table has an equal vote". "You've got to be kidding", he said. No, she said. He got up and walked out.

But it's fundamental to have teachers the kids want to learn with, Thomas says. "The kids are going to decide in 15 minutes whether to let you live or eat you alive. We need to know who the kids will learn from".

Each student chooses the teacher s/he want as an adviser. Different teachers

---

[11]"I have never felt disrespected in this school by any student at any time", says one of the founding teachers at Avalon.

appeal to different students, and this provides some flexibility. But if a teacher is not chosen by enough students, over a long enough period of time, there will be a question within the co-operative whether that teacher should stay. There have been cases where the co-operative has had to deal with that, and has.

2. To reallocate expenditures and contain costs

Minnesota like other states has been struggling to protect revenue for program and class size. K-12 is a labor-intensive model and the organized teachers are able politically to move up their salaries. Settlement by settlement the districts overspend, then cut program and increase class size. After which, blaming the Legislature for "not giving us enough", the districts go either to their local voters or back to the next legislative session for revenue to "close the budget gap". But the state has not got unlimited resources either, for what already represents by far the largest single item in its budget. As it stands, relying so largely on the technology of teacher-talk, it is not a sustainable model.

In theory the board balances the teachers' interest in compensation with the parents' and students' interest in program. But in reality the boards, convinced they can never win a strike, have decided it is better to buy peace, to settle.[12] The students can't strike. And there is the hope that the threat of cutting out the extracurricular activities or raising class size will activate the parents to work to increase revenue next year.

In 2001 the Minnesota Legislature changed the financing for Minnesota public education. It shifted the base revenue to state-raised non-property sources, for which K-12 would henceforth have to compete against other state functions. It left the district free to get additional revenue from the local property tax but required the district to persuade the voters to agree to the excess levy. These new 'rules of the game' caused one Twin Cities area superintendent to speculate, for the first time since I'd known him, about an effort to deal with the cost side, about "getting our unit costs down". He could see what that would involve: increasing the use of aides and paraprofessionals, increasing the use of 'technology', ending the requirement that the youngest and lowest-cost teachers must be laid off first. But he could see no way to get there. All these changes run through the teachers. And, under traditional arrangements the teachers have no reason to agree to such changes.

In November 1999 officials from the sponsoring LeSueur district came to Henderson for the annual discussion about the school's year: Harold Larson, the

---

[12]I knew one board chair who said she couldn't stand, emotionally, to get involved with the bargaining. "Just tell me when it's done", she said, "how much".

superintendent; Virginia Miller, the board chair; two other members of the sitting board; and two newly elected members not yet seated. For New Country and EdVisions there were the chair of the board of the school, teachers on the board, and others in the EdVisions co-operative. The EdVisions people reported the school ended the year in the black. There had been a salary review. Some teachers received raises and some did not.

This puzzled the two newly-elected board members, the district having not yet settled its contract with its teachers. They asked the board chair how it was possible. He said he didn't know: The board (at the school) doesn't make the compensation decisions. This puzzled the two new district board members even more.

The EdVisions people tried to explain: the arrangement, the process, the rationale. Finally one of the teachers looked at the new district board members and said, "We had to ask ourselves: How could we tell the kids they weren't going to get an upgrade in their software next year because we wanted to take out more in salary for ourselves?"

Teachers at Henderson in fact have salaries higher than they would in comparable jobs in nearby districts. They work hard, accept non-teaching assignments with the co-operative (usually with extra pay). This in a school that—like most chartered schools—does not get some of the categorical aids that come to a school in the district sector.

In this arrangement the group of teachers is responsible for balancing internally the interests of program and compensation. If it doesn't pay its members well the school won't have teachers, and will close. If it doesn't maintain program the school won't keep students, and will close. A chartered school has no local voters to go to for an excess levy. So a tradeoff has to be made. And within the cooperative or partnership framework it tends to be made with integrity.[13]

3. To get professional status for teachers

The unions have been talking about getting teachers into control of the decisions about the how the school teaches, and who does what, especially since Albert Shanker's initiative after *A Nation at Risk*. Traditionally these roles have not been open to teachers: Management decides how school runs. Gene Mammenga, when lobbyist for the Minnesota Education Association, would say when people complained the unions were obsessed with economic issues: "We argue about salaries and benefits because that's all you let us argue about". Boards do not have to bargain

---

[13]By contrast, the process at the district level often fails to make the tradeoff with integrity. In this adversarial process the union argues the teachers' interests and the board in theory defends the public's and the students' interests. See page 45.

professional issues and the unions so far have not been able to persuade legislatures to require them to do so.

In the discussion group convened in 1985 by then-Gov. Rudy Perpich Greg Burns initially represented the Minnesota Federation of Teachers. He argued hard for teachers being allowed to control professional issues. In the decade since bargaining had come into law, he said, the unions and the districts had fought to a stand-off. The unions had won their members most of the bread-and-butter issues. But the boards had been able to protect the area of professional issues as a management right. All this had gotten locked into law, into regulation, into master contracts, into court rulings and into arbitrators' decisions.

We should move decisions to schools, Burns argued, where all these questions could be taken up anew and the roles and relationships rethought.

The response especially from the school boards association was to ask: If the decisions about the learning program were turned over to teachers in the school, how would they be accountable? To this Burns could only say: Trust us. This was, not surprisingly, unpersuasive. Any such deal depends on the teachers being willing to offer something real in return by way of accountability. And the employment model within the bureau arrangement provides no way to do that.

Discussion continues about teachers getting into professional issues. But there is little progress. The kids who were in kindergarten when Burns was appealing to the Governor's Discussion Group were graduating by the time Louise Sundin, the Minneapolis local president, negotiated the contract in 1997 that was supposed to start teachers into professional roles.

Boards of education are determined not to lose control of their last 'management right'. If we lose this, the MSBA lobbyist said to its summer conference in 1998, boards will have no role left. Others might dispute that; might say that boards would do better to focus on objectives and on results. Perhaps that's true. But at the moment this is not the way boards see it. The positions are frozen in the boss/worker framework.

Teacher-ownership, especially in a charter context, offers a way around this stand-off, offers a new deal in which by offering real accountability teachers get professional roles in return.

One of the fastest-growing realty firms in America, Counselor Realty, is owned by its professionals. The realtors in its offices elect their own managers. They take not only their own commissions but also what in a conventional realty firm is the owner's profit. One of its owner-members, and the elected manager of its Wayzata office, was Peg Swanson, in 1997–99 president of the Minnesota School Boards

Association. In this arrangement the professionals stay much longer than realtors in conventional firms. Low turnover low means low training costs. Longer experience means a better knowledge of the market. The worker-owners take the rewards.

4. To strengthen school leadership

The idea of teacher ownership has significant implications also for the question of school leadership.

By the late '90s K-12 was having considerable trouble finding and holding both superintendents and principals. 'Leadership' became an issue. Foundations moved in with substantial efforts to help identify, recruit and train leaders, especially school leaders, since the pressing need was felt to be to "improve instruction".

The question of leadership changes dramatically if you pull out the assumption of teacher-employment and substitute a professional model. In a professional model there is a dual structure of leadership: a partner responsible for professional issues and an administrator responsible for operations. And the relationship between the two is different than in a school where the teachers work for administrators. In other fields the professionals have the administrators working for them. Compensation is different, too. Partners in other fields may earn three times what the administrator earns. "In the district the superintendent is paid twice the top professional," a teacher commented at the end of a look at the parallels between education and the professions (and before the cap came off superintendent salaries in Minnesota).

5. To get 'learning technology' into the schools

Until the early '90s it was generally accepted that the best way to put young people in touch with the world of information was to send into their classroom a well-trained teacher with good books under her arm.

Today that is no longer true. No teacher, no matter how well trained, no matter what the books under her arm, can bring students the breadth and depth of information now available to them through the Internet and the World Wide Web. Tim Berners-Lee wrote the code for the web in 1991. Within a decade there have appeared . . . what? 20 million sites? 30 million? 40 million? The scope and suddenness of this change is beyond almost anything we have experienced.

At the first anniversary of the Saint Paul Saturn School in 1992 Albert Shanker could see the need. European countries sort and track their students much more than we do, he said. From fifth grade on the American teacher is confronted with a mixed-ability classroom. This creates a dilemma. Spend more time with the quicker kids and pretty soon you have big drop-out and discipline problems with the slower kids. Spend more time with the slower kids and pretty soon you're hearing from the parents of the brighter and now-not-challenged kids. Individualization is the answer. Yet we can't provide a teacher for every kid. Technology, which lets kids interact with learning at their own pace, he could see, is the way out.

I went one day in the late '80s to an elementary school in the Osseo district to watch a demonstration of some company's computer software. The computer was not working right, and I'd always found it unsatisfying anyway to stand around watching someone else use a program. So I drifted out into the hall, just as a class of third-graders was filing into the computer lab next door. I stood in the doorway, watching and listening. The person handling the lab was standing close to me, but said nothing. The teacher was busy with her students.

The Apple II machines were on four rows of tables. The capacity of the central processor was limited, so the teacher had the rows of students take turns. Row A, hit this key. Then, Row B, hit this key. It went on like that, the teacher moving each row of students from key to key.

In front of me a little girl in Row D hit a key. The boy next to her leaned over and whispered, "You shouldn't have done that." The teacher, walking by Row D, saw the girl had hit that key. Without saying a word she pulled the girl's chair back from the table. The little girl put her head down and her hands in her lap.

It went on. Row A, hit this key. Row B, hit this key. Pretty soon the teacher was back at Row D. She leaned down and said something in the little girl's ear. The girl nodded. The teacher pushed her chair back up to the table. Then continued: Row A, hit this key . . .

The lab attendant saw me taking this in. She seemed to feel she should make some comment. She stepped over to me and said, "This little girl has been a problem. She likes to work ahead."

The point here has to do not with computer labs—schools have of course moved way beyond Apple IIs—but with the impulse to force the new equipment into the old classroom methods, with the teacher controlling 'instruction'.

Joe Graba, who has been the dean of the Graduate School of Education at Hamline University and a consultant on technology to the Midwest Higher Education Commission, thinks the New Country School makes the best use of learning hardware and software of any school he has seen. It does not use learning programs, does not do courses even on disk or online. The computers are the students' connection to all the resources available through the Internet and on the web. The computers are connected all day long. The server is in the school. The students run the server. The school does not teach about computers. The kids simply tell each other how.

States are voting the money to wire the schools, to connect to the web. The education industry is trying hard to sell the districts hardware and software. But the superintendent cannot make the teachers change their practice. The principal cannot make the teachers do it. As Jim Walker, a former Minnesota Superintendent of the Year, used to say about change in general: "Management cannot do it. Only the teachers can do it."

But even teachers cannot do it without the right incentives, without reasons and opportunities to change the way they practice. Ownership—the opportunity for the professional group to take responsibility for student success and to benefit if it can produce that success—creates those incentives. Some people sniff at governance changes as irrelevant to what teachers do. No: Not if these are changes that radically alter the structure of opportunity and reward in ways that at last align the teachers' interest with the objectives of improving student learning.

PART THREE

WHAT WILL IT TAKE TO GET IT DONE?

Chapter 10

WORK THROUGH THE POWER OF STATE LAWMAKING

To make public education a self-improving institution the country will absolutely need to work through the power of state lawmaking.

The problem is in the system. The system—the rules of the game—exists in state law. Problems of system design require changing state law. The legislature is the architect of the system. So those in state policy leadership are the critical actors.

The national government needs to see that it can and should move through the process of state lawmaking to accomplish its own goals. The national government has decreed that public education must improve and has threatened consequences if it does not. But its threat will be effective only as the institution responds. As presently arranged the institution cannot respond adequately. For there to be an adequate response the national government will need the states to change present arrangements.

The Constitution of the United States does not make education a responsibility of the national government. Matters not expressly delegated to the national government are reserved to the states. The constitutions of the states assign the responsibility for public education to the legislature, charge it to establish by statute a "general and uniform" and/or "thorough and efficient" system of schools. Florida was an exception, in assigning responsibility constitutionally to its counties until this was changed in 1998. In Colorado the courts continue to debate how far the Legislature can override 'local control'.

Much of the discussion about the schools is either local or national. So quite naturally people think in terms of acting locally or acting nationally. But if we are serious about improvement we will need to get the fundamentals right. And the reality is that neither local action nor national action can significantly change the fundamentals that cause the institution to behave as it does.

The states have been busy on an education agenda, of course, ever since the 1983 publication of *A Nation at Risk*. Early, most state efforts, too, were directed at getting the existing institution to do-better. But in the '90s the states began moving to change system-arrangements. This is imperative. It is too great a risk for the states to continue to rely exclusively on the districts being willing and able to improve existing schools enough and quickly enough. The states cannot wait indefinitely for the districts to get it done, or go on indefinitely trying to push improvements into the districts from the outside.

Before explaining what the states should do it will be useful to explain why neither local nor national action can do what needs to be done.

Local action can't change the system

In the late 1980s the Institute for Educational Leadership, as part of a series of studies about local boards, organized a project to help selected cities restructure the governance of their public education.

An advisory committee was formed. Early in its discussions the question was raised whether communities actually can change the governance of their public education. The question was noted. Work began and for a time the project made progress. Two or three interested cities were identified and discussions were opened with their leadership. But quickly the effort slowed. Soon the project quietly disappeared.

Reality had asserted itself: Communities cannot change the basic arrangements for the governance of education. There is no concept of home rule in American public education. Municipal governments won the right a century ago to decide their own form of government. And in the 1970s counties got substantial home-rule powers for county government. But there is still no process under which citizens can draft a new plan for local K-12 education, put it to a vote and, if it is approved, operate under the new and locally-determined institutional arrangement. In 1995 the legislature in Texas set up a kind of process for district home-rule, but as of 2004 it remained unused.

The school district is a creature of state law. Locally the board can change the district's internal organization; its own board structure and its administration. But it cannot change the rules by which it plays. It cannot change its powers and duties or the number of members on its board; cannot move, say, from electing members at-large to electing members by districts. Questions about changing the structure and powers of public education go to the legislature in each state. Sometimes this is for a change in the general provisions of law applying to all districts. Often it is for a local bill applying to a particular district. State legislation, general or special, is the way the structure of public education is changed in America. If improvement requires restructuring the system—as it does—state legislation is required for improvement.

This is often hard for people to see and to accept. At a meeting at a major New York foundation in the late 1980s a well-known corporate CEO was incredulous at the suggestion that those concerned to improve the schools in New York City should work for changes in state law. "The people who run the New York schools are in New York City; we're in New York City. Why would we want to talk to Albany?"

In recent years people have come to understand the need to "talk to Albany". In 2002 the new mayor of New York City, Michael Bloomberg, went to the state to get the change in law abolishing the city board of education and transferring control of the schools to the mayor. This left still a single corporation; simply changed the leadership of it. But even this did require action by the state.

The failure to see or to accept the need for the state to change the basic arrangements for public education has serious consequences. It causes people to keep on doing things that are not effective, causes them to keep on pushing buttons not connected to live wires. It leads people away from the real system-changes that would be effective.

We need to be clear. The problem of defective incentives is in state law. Local action cannot change state law. So local action cannot cure the underlying problem.

National action can't remake the system

Those who move on a national stage—journalists, scholars, policy advocates, some foundations, officials in national office—want to be seen doing something about a problem the public cares about. So they offer ideas, plead for and promise action. The notion is that a problem occurring everywhere in the country must have a national solution; meaning, action by the national government. Too few ask whether national action can be effective.[1]

The conventional assumption—that a very large problem requires a large organization to deal with it—is misleading. Often the larger the problem the more important it is to get a large number of small actors each doing a little. Think about the energy crises of the 1970s, relieved in the end not by a single action to increase energy supply but by a large number of small local and private actions that were driven by incentives to reduce energy use.

In areas of domestic policy that are a national concern, but that exist under state law and are constitutionally beyond its reach, the national government often tries to

---

[1]Delegations from other countries can be seriously confused when they come to Washington to compare 'national' policies for education. Those who arrange international exchanges sometimes fail to make clear that in areas of domestic policy such as education the counterpart of the European national government, of the European 'state', is the American state government.

act through its power to appropriate money and to impose regulations on the use of that money. Members of Congress and officials in the executive branch long ago came to the idea of hanging requirements onto the categorical-grant programs as a way of 'doing something' in policy areas their legislation cannot reach directly. The assumption is that the states will never reject the aid, so will accept any regulations attached to it. That is the approach built into No Child Left Behind.

But if it is to work the new law will need help that only the states can provide. The law does change some of the rules of the game for the K-12 institution. It introduces measurements and promises consequences. It essentially commands improvement. It assumes that the various parts of the institution will then comply; will adjust and adapt, change and improve, accordingly. But the schools and districts must have the capacity to adapt and to improve.

Unless they can change, the incentive for the districts will be to defy the law and to press the states not to comply. This resistance could be effective. The states were offended by the national government using its seven per cent contribution to K-12, in a period when the states' finances were tight, to coerce them into compliance. By 2004 states' resistance was visibly rising. This will increasingly test the national government's willingness to enforce the consequences. And the states are aware the government may not hold the cards it needs. They know that before 2002, as the lobbyist for the National Conference of State Legislatures wrote, the federal government almost never withheld any education money from any state.

If things proceed along this course the new initiative for improvement will suffer the fate of the National Goals effort that emerged from the first presidential education summit in 1989. None of the goals was accomplished. The new accountability apparatus could fall of its own weight. Such things have happened. The national government, as a veteran Minnesota congressman says, is not incapable of "screwing it up".

A little history may be instructive.

A mandate that failed: The case of metropolitan growth

In the 1960s and '70s the national government tried to use the 'requirements' approach to achieve the goal of orderly development and management of the nation's metropolitan areas—another major area of domestic policy constitutionally the responsibility of the states.

America was increasingly an urban nation. The regions were living, growing entities with nobody explicitly in charge of planning and managing their life-support systems: energy supply, waste disposal, transport, housing, public safety, communications, water supply, land-use and the environment. There was no public body responsible for raising and resolving their large, strategic issues or for balancing the development of the suburban fringe and the redevelopment of the urban core. Their municipalities' dependence on the local property tax worked powerfully to distort development and to create inequities in service levels and tax burdens. So urban growth became 'a national problem'. And in the days of The New Frontier and The Great Society the national government tried to act, moved to take control.

Federal legislation could not reach the major elements of the urban system, however. The structure of local government and its financing, the property tax, the laws governing land use and development, housing construction and housing occupancy—most all the public elements of the urban system—exist in state law. So the federal government moved to attach planning requirements to its programs of aid for urban development and re-development.

In 1966 Congress required that plans for roads, transit, parks, sewer and water systems, housing, airports, urban renewal and local planning be consistent with an adopted regional plan. And required that regional planning bodies be established to develop the plans and to review all requests for federal aid in order to ensure that projects conformed to these plans. The makeup of these regional clearing-houses was specified in the national law. Failure to comply would result in the loss of aid. From this structure and process, the theory of action solemnly pronounced, orderly metropolitan development would proceed.

It was a disaster. Washington politics dictated that the regional planning mechanisms be constructed as "councils of governments", composed of persons serving in elected municipal and county office. This asked local officials whose property-tax revenues depended on getting development to locate within their own boundaries to think and act in the larger, regional interest. Interests and objectives were misaligned.

The result was predictable. The city and county officials were no way going to put their federal aid at risk because a project "did not conform to the regional plan". Nor were these local officials going to support regional decision-making about development. They did of course want the money. So they faked it. The regional clearinghouses became what David Walker of the Advisory Commission on Inter-governmental Relations called "paper mills", routinely approving almost every application. Some never found any project that did not conform to the regional plan, or never developed a plan to which projects proposed by its local-government members would not conform.

There was nothing, really, that the national government could do. The whole effort was shut down by the new administration that came into office in 1981. Quickly the regional-planning apparatus withered. Functioning regional management and planning institutions survived mainly in a few metropolitan areas where they had been established in state law: the Twin Cities area of Minnesota, perhaps Atlanta and the San Francisco Bay Area.

There's a risk in believing you can nationalize change

There is probably a lesson in this for the national government today as it tries to affect public education in the states. Only so much can be accomplished through requirements, and the 'big stick' of withholding aids may turn out to be made of balsa wood.

System change has no power base, no constituency in Washington. On the question of urban policy the power in Washington was in the associations of local officials: the National League of Cities, the U.S. Conference of Mayors and the National Association of Counties, all determined to oppose an approach to metropolitan organization that did not put their members in charge. There was no countervailing lobby for the regional approach. So inevitably the mechanism created to make the regional decisions was, not to put too fine a point on it, not well aligned with the goal the legislation was intended to accomplish.

The same danger exists now for the effort to change K-12 education.

The national capital has become the preferred location for the power groups in education, as for the lobbies in almost every group in almost every field with an interest in protecting the status quo. Washington is their headquarters and the focus of their lobbying efforts. It is not smart to bring into that political setting proposals for change radical enough to offend the power groups so influential both in Congress and with the executive branch.

It is true that in 1994 in its new program of federal aid for the start-up of chartered schools the national government did, remarkably, agree to respect state law with respect to the schools and sponsors to be eligible. But this was a stroke of luck that depended largely on the Clinton administration having decided to support the charter idea and on the initiative of Minnesota's Senator Dave Durenberger. Despite the lurking hostility of the interest groups Congress did agree the federal government would conform. But it is never wise to depend on the presence of individuals who can be gone overnight. Certainly it is not smart to put the entire strategy at risk in that way. You may have made it home successfully once through a dark alley in a dangerous part of town at 3 a.m. But getting by with it once does not make it a good idea as a regular practice.

There is an important role for the national government, to be sure, in policy leadership. But probably the best course is for the president to move proposals into the process of state lawmaking where the control over institutional arrangements really lies.

National policy can use state lawmaking

The American state legislature is better than its reputation. It is to be sure a political institution, a marketplace in which adults make deals. And like the Congress it has become unattractively partisan in recent years. But it carries a serious responsibility for establishing, maintaining and revising the complex arrangements for the institutions of modern public life. The state's primary job is not to make the operating decisions, for the cities or for the schools. Its primary job is large-system architecture: to create the institutions that make the decisions and to structure properly the incentives that will shape their organizations' behavior.

Most state legislatures are quite productive, meeting only a part of the year (a few still only every other year) yet turning out far more work than the Congress. The state legislature is fiscally responsible in a way the national legislature is not: Unlike Congress it does not have the option of deficit finance, of printing money. There is truth to the old saw about the making of law resembling the making of sausage: best not to watch it up close. But so is there in the wisdom about judging a legislature only in retrospect, in terms of what it has accomplished.

Since 1985 the states have changed the system of public education quite remarkably. And the governors and legislators enacting open enrollment and the chartering laws did not have behind them grass-roots support or a huge wave of media attention. Usually these laws were state capitol policy initiatives, championed by a governor or a few legislators who understood the problems in K-12 and the need for radical change, often at the urging of a few local supporters and by advocates like Joe Nathan, from the Center for School Change at the University of Minnesota, who were in many states. These officials had to act against the opposition of powerful groups that, all conventional political wisdom predicted, would kill any such initiative.

But the initiatives succeeded. Legislators such as Ember Reichgott Junge, Ken Nelson, Becky Kelso, Mindy Greiling and Alice Seagren in Minnesota; Gary Hart in California; Wib Gulley in North Carolina, Dwight Evans in Pennsylvania; Jim Argue in Arkansas; Joe Tedder, as a freshman House member in Florida; Joe Doria and Jack Ewing, old pros from the opposite sides of the political fence in New Jersey; Cooper Snyder and Mike Fox in Ohio; governors as skillful and as determined as Rudy Perpich in Minnesota when pushing open enrollment in 1985; Roy Romer in Colorado, Tommy Thompson in Wisconsin, John Engler in Michigan, Tom Ridge in Pennsylvania and later Arne Carlson in Minnesota . . . and more. Those who carried the charter bills took big risks. It was surprisingly bipartisan. Altogether it has been an astonishing policy initiative and far more radical than anything from the national government.

The changes being worked by legislators testify to "the necessary in-competence of the politician". The late Senator Hubert Humphrey was charmed by this notion when he encountered it in Europe in the mid-1960s from those who built the supra-national institutions of Western Europe. None of the experts would have proposed such an initiative, knowing it could not possibly succeed. 'Politicians', not knowing it could not be done, did it.

Might national leadership connect itself to this process of state lawmaking?[2]

A president's advisers are reluctant to think in these terms. There are 50 states. It is a federal system. The tendency is to say, as William Galston on the staff of the Domestic Policy Council said in the mid-'90s, "We don't control the states". (Neither, of course, given the separation of powers, does the president necessarily control Congress, even when the House and Senate are of the president's party.) And the agencies handling domestic policy do not think in terms of diplomacy. They think in terms of law and regulation. The impulse in the national agencies is to work directly with their counterpart agencies in the states, bypassing the policy process at the state level and leveraging off of the states' desire not to give up federal aid. They lack (and make little effort to get) disinterested field intelligence.[3]

But the state-based strategy is possible. Nothing in the Constitution requires a president to speak only to the Congress or prohibits a president from making proposals to the legislatures of the states. With both levels of policymaking much can be done with negotiation, with diplomacy. Certainly much could be done, by a president so inclined.

The central realities are compelling. The improvement of public education is a high national priority. The institution cannot significantly improve as presently structured. Its system must be changed. The levers that control what needs to be changed are in the states. Common sense suggests the national government should now get beyond its minimally effective efforts to command through regulation. It

---

[2]The national government requires the standards and assessments to be enacted by state legislatures; something it feels entitled to do in return for the aid it provides. The question beyond this is whether the national government will push the legislatures to change basic system arrangements. Interestingly, references in the national law to the 'charter schools' assumes the presence of a state chartering law.

[3]A conceivable response—if agencies such as the Department of Education are not inclined to activate the process of state lawmaking—is to give the responsibility in these policy areas to a domestic equivalent of the Department of State. 'State' understands diplomacy; thinks in terms of getting things done without the power to command. American diplomacy was more successful in reconstructing the governmental institutions of Western Europe after World War II than was the Department of Housing and Urban Development in reconstructing the governmental institutions in the metropolitan regions of America.

should intervene constructively and skillfully to get state policy leadership to create in law the new open sector of public education in which there is the capacity to start different schools new. National policy will depend on state lawmaking.

Recap: The action agenda for the states

◼ *Use common sense about 'standards'*

Lots of questions remain to be settled about the accountability model as a driver of improvement. Good legislation takes time, often years: Not all decisions are made well the first time through. Often some early decisions do need to be re-thought. Some rethinking is normal.

The current effort is to use requirements linked to federal aid to force districts to improve performance in existing schools, tightening these requirements gradually over time as the politics permit. The argument is that the groups affected will always resist but will never win. Still, this runs against the old wisdom about not issuing orders that will not or cannot be obeyed. Even under pressure the districts might not be able significantly to improve performance in exising schools within existing arrangements.

A common-sense effort to make sure K-12 is willing and able to respond begins with the question of standards. Having standards is now essential, is accepted. The country is no longer 'in the opportunity business'. But the determination to ensure performance is one thing, the question of what specifically students are to know and be able to do is another.

The issues about this involve mainly secondary school. In these years students have traditionally been taught subjects. The different aspects of the real situations students will find in life are divided in high school into 'disciplines'; into courses offered at different times, as students will find knowledge divided when they move into higher education. This may not represent the best learning. The qualification of teachers is defined as their ability to teach courses in subjects. High scores on subject-matter tests have come to be defined as 'success'. This is partly because the practical requirements for multiple-choice questions and short written answers force the curriculum toward the kind of learning most easily tested, and because scores are so easy for the media to report and for the public to understand.

That is not necssarily the answer we want. It suffers from what Whitehead called the "fatal unconnectedness" of academic disciplines. It risks driving schooling into a uniform model, leaving no room for different schools in which teachers are better motivated to teach well and in which students are better motivated to learn well.

Sensible state leadership, recognizing the differences among students, should—and likely will—leave room for schools built on different models. Legislators and governors are realistic, and do understand that the discussion about standards is driven heavily by adult interests. They will need both to filter-out the adult interests and to develop a stronger sense of fairness in the way the decisions treat students.

The economic interest of adults is obvious. In secondary school, where teachers teach subjects, the decision about what kids have to learn determines who teaches, and therefore who has a job. About 1985, lobbying that Erling Johnson described as the most intense in his experience while commissioner of education and later as a member of the state board defeated, 4–3, a proposal to raise the requirements for math and science in Minnesota junior high schools. The lobbying came from the teachers of electives.

The ideological interests parallel the economic. In 2004 in the Minnesota Legislature there was clearly a Republican and a DFL (Democratic) version of American history, fought over in the course of adopting standards for high school social science. The disagreements come also out of differences in learning philosophy. Many adults are deeply committed to subject-matter learning, to courses and classes and to coverage. Others disagree; think school should train young people how to think critically, how to reason well, how to understand the different considerations involved in a given situation.[4]

The trouble is that at the moment the assumption that high school is courses is seldom questioned. It needs to be questioned. There really is more than one respectable idea about how to engage students in the hard work of learning. Courses-and-classes will work for some and not for others. Some students will do better and will be far more motivated by project-based learning, by school that offers them the opportunity to study particular situations in all their reality. John Gardner, the former Secretary of Health, Education and Welfare once wrote: "All too often we are giving young people cut flowers when we should be teaching them to grow their own . . . We think of the mind as a storehouse to be filled rather than as an instrument to be used".[5] We do not know for sure what will work with all students. Much as this might trouble traditionalists, it is possible that individualization is 'best practice'. Certainly we need to try different things. Trying-things should be the theme for state policy in the current situation.

---

[4]"Which does not mean, as some traditionalists sometimes suggest, courses on "How To Think Critically".

[5]*No Easy Victories*, Harper&Row, 1969, Chapter 12.

In their decisions about standards the states also need to be fair. There is an uncomfortable sense in the discussion that once standards are set and consequences are clear all students should perform. And that those who fail will deserve to fail. Those who care about kids believe it is deeply unfair for adults, ignoring the differences in human ability, to impose that kind of failure on young people just getting started in life. This was Gov. Rudy Perpich's view. When pressed by the business community to support a testing initiative for Minnesota in the mid-1980s he resisted. "I've seen too many people who passed tests and failed life," he told associates. "And too many people who failed tests and passed life. I'm not going to make testing that important."

This is an issue the states need to consider, and resolve. Probably not many people at the moment have this issue about standards at the top of their agenda for state action. They should. In the discussion the policy leadership should listen to students about this question which affects them so profoundly.[6]

▪ *Do not try to run the schools*

In the 1980s the idea appeared that failing districts should be taken over and run by the state. New Jersey took over Newark, and after that Paterson and Jersey City. There were also takeovers in the Midwest and on the West Coast. In 1995 when yet another superintendent quit after yet another failed effort at improving internally, the state of Ohio took over Cleveland. In 1998, frustrated by the district, Pennsylvania put in law a process for taking over Philadelphia.

The illusion persists that it is possible to change 'the system' if you control 'the system'. The risk, perhaps the reality, is that when you control the system you become the system. Mayors may want to take the risk: There are reasons to want to be in charge that do not involve reform. But certainly the state should resist the temptation.

In recent years the enthusiasm for state takeover has waned. Commissioners like Thomas Sobol in New York never did warm to the idea of becoming superintendent of a collection of the lowest-performing districts in the state. It was more appealing to think of the state getting somebody else to do what the district could not do well. "That's a fertile idea for me", Sobol said.

Asked what it meant for New Jersey to take over Newark an adviser to then-Gov. James Florio, Tom Corcoran, said: "We sent in four people". Corcoran saw clearly the fundamental problem with takeover; that on taking over the state did

---

[6]See Chapter 13.

not have much more ability to change the district than did the superintendent hired by the local board. Some states got in and fairly quickly got out. Ohio got out quickly, preferring to turn over Cleveland to its mayor. New Jersey has not yet extricated itself from its takeover districts.

Long-term, state takeover is in the interest neither of the public nor of the state itself. "When the state takes over", Corcoran said, "there is nobody left to be critical".

■ Create a 'somebody else' to offer public education

The essential action for the state is to remove the public-utility arrangement that traps local boards of education in a conflict of interest that paralyzes their ability to do what is essential for improvement. This is critical now for public education in the core cities.

The idea that in any community there could be only a single organization offering public education grew up in a time when cities were small and when the real city and the legal city were one and the same. As development spilled over the original municipal boundary, as suburbs appeared, the notion of the single organization for the whole community was destroyed. In the suburbs there were many, often small, districts. But in the central city the concept persisted of a single organization no matter how large. This left bureaucratic organizations trying to educate 400,000 students, 600,000 students, 1,000,000 students, many in families that cannot afford to move. It has proved very difficult for anyone, even the state, to change these big organizations.

For the state, having only one organization makes no basic sense, gives it no leverage to improve education where education most needs to be improved. So, prudently, the states are now moving to hedge the bet, withdrawing the district's traditional exclusive on public education in the community and empowering other entities to create new schools. These alternate sponsors now exist in many states. Some, such as the separate chartering board in Arizona or the colleges and universities able to charter schools in some states, are statewide in their jurisdiction. Others are local: In authorizing the City of Milwaukee and the City of Indianapolis to charter new schools, state policy leadership in Wisconsin and Indiana has created in effect a second 'education board' for the city.

■ Convert school boards into 'education boards'

Frustrated by the difficulty of changing their existing schools, some superintendents and boards of education in big districts are now considering starting—probably chartering—new schools; creating an open sector internal to the district. The state should encourage this impulse where it appears.

It is not easy, however, for a local board to oversee a split operation, with some of its schools owned and operated directly and with some on contract. So states may want to consider intervening—in a big city, for example—to divest the board of its owned schools entirely, creating what the Education Commission of the States has been calling 'an all-charter district'.

It was the state, after all, that set up the districts in the own-and-operate model. So the state created the problem for the boards, is responsible for the requirement that their members serve both as the board setting policy on behalf of the community and simultaneously as the board of the 'operating company' owning and running the schools. The state has the responsibility for fixing the problem it created. And the state is entitled to do this. An official in New York describes that state's big-city districts as 'dysfunctional'. A state should not have to tolerate dysfunctional organizations for the carrying-out of a state constitutional responsibility as important as public education.

It is appealing to think of the boards themselves resolving this conflict by delegating operations to their owned schools, making these autonomous and accountable where they are now not-autonomous and not-accountable. And from time to time some study group does recommend that school boards function as policy boards. But this is naïve: Boards probably are going to feel entitled to run schools that in fact they own. They are deeply into control, and are unlikely to give this up voluntarily. If the state wants the boards not to think like operators it will have to structure them out of owning the schools.

Do a divestiture, even!

The state is Zeus: It can throw a lightning bolt. A state that wants the dynamics created when improvement is school-based can by law take the board out of the school-running business, moving the board into a buyer role with respect to its existing schools. A state could do this for all districts. Or just for some; for its big districts, for example. Or just for districts not performing well.

States have been playing Zeus as they have intervened in cities to restructure the board or to abolish the board and put the responsibility for education under the mayor. But these are variations on the old strategy of 'firing the coach'. Divestiture is different. It is not changing-the-people-in-charge. It is more radical. It drops the administrative bureau model. Whoever is in charge—the board or the mayor—would oversee schools run by others; would be responsible not for operations but for resources and for results.[7]

---

[7]In England and Wales in 1988 the schools were substantially taken out of the control of the local authorities (districts) and made autonomous. This reform was left in place by the Labor government that took office in 1997. The reform, and the research about its effects, is summarized in Julian Le Grand, *Motivation, Agency and Public Policy*, Oxford University Press, 2003, Chapter 8.

Divestiture can take different forms.

- Each individual school could go on a contract with the board.
- At the other extreme, the state could spin off the entire existing district administration—as it stands, with its existing employee contracts—into a single public entity operating under an agreement with the board.
- Or the state could break down the old administration into some number of such entities, each on contract to the board to run, say, a third or a quarter of the schools. Note that this is not the geographic breakup that is almost everywhere rejected. Rather, the state would break up (better, break down) the district nongeographically. Each operating group would offer its program district-wide, giving parents in each part of the city some choice of learning program.
- The state could design and install such a divestiture itself, as Pennsylvania did (or started to do) for Philadelphia. Or the state could simply require that the local board plan and implement a divestiture by a date-certain, the state reserving the right to impose the divestiture itself if the locals fail to act.

And so forth. There are always more shoes in the back room than the salesman tells you there are.

■ *Create a leadership agency at the state level too*

As the states introduce the new opportunities for schools to be created new, both outside the district sector and within it, a question will arise about the arrangements for the oversight of education at the state level and especially in the executive branch.

Typically there is now a department of education overseen by a commissioner (in some places 'state superintendent'). Sometimes this state education agency is responsible to a state board but more often now it relates directly to the governor. The tendency of any bureaucracy is to see itself maintaining the state of affairs entrusted to it, and these agencies have not been conspicuous for their support of change and innovation.[8] Their job is to administer programs, to adopt and enforce rules, to distribute funds. Most get a large part of their revenue from the national government, to oversee its grant programs. They tend as a result not to be notably flexible. Few if any are policy-entrepreneurial—though in the late 1990s a few state commissioners took a membership in the Education Leaders Council in place of (or in addition to) their membership in the more 'establishment' Council of Chief State School Officers.

---

[8]Studies by Tim Mazzoni when at the University of Minnesota College of Education made clear that major policy initiatives in Minnesota have almost always arisen outside the department.

The states probably will need to develop separate oversight agencies for the district sector and for the innovative sector, the open sector. The entity overseeing the open sector will need to have a different culture: more flexible, more entrepreneurial, more performance-oriented. The national government now has an Office of Innovation and Improvement, and one of Minnesota Gov. Tim Pawlenty's early acts in 2003 was to create a Division of Choice and Innovation within the Minnesota Department of Education. Perhaps in time the states will create separate agencies for the two sectors.

The challenge is to change the way people think

The new strategy has created a new situation that does not fit the old picture people carry in their heads about public education. Suddenly public education is more than the district and its schools. As a result there is now a visible difference between the interest of the students, in getting to the schools they believe will serve them best, and the interest of the districts in holding on to students and the money that comes with them. People struggle—newspaper reporters do, business groups and others do—to decide what to think about this new world. Is this good? Is this bad? What interest is most important: The district's? The students'? Where is now the public interest?

The states' move to unbundle the K-12 institution is generating resistance. As districts feel the new strategy taking hold they increasingly try to blame the district's financial troubles on open enrollment, the chartered schools, the state's whole program for bringing choices to students. They pressure the state to put a stop to this. Legislators are realistic about the districts' self-interest. But that does not make the politics easier to handle.

Like so many political struggles this one is very largely a struggle about ideas. Increasingly, success requires a major effort to change the way people think.

Chapter 11

THINK CLEARLY

The opposition to the states' program of new schools counts on keeping influential groups committed to the old ideas used to support the regulated-public-utility arrangement of K-12 education. Developing an open sector in public education will require state policy leadership to challenge and to change those old ideas.

The new-schools effort will require good politics, of course—and leadership and organization and financing, much skill and some luck. But, while necessary, these are never sufficient where action requires changing the way people think. It is essential to win the battle of ideas; is essential to deal effectively with the arguments thrown up by those resisting change. Journalists and others who think politics is simply money and people and power underestimate how heavily it is about ideas, and how far success turns on the ability to explain and to persuade; to educate.

The forces defending the established order of things are skilled at deflecting the pressures for change. They know how to shape their arguments in ways that hide the self-interest beneath. They know how difficult change of any sort is to sell and offer endless reasons why people should stick with the way things are.

Those proposing change have a harder job, and those proposing to change basic system-arrangements have the hardest job of all. They have to explain that the problem is not bad people or insufficient financing but the defective rules of the game; have to explain how systems work and why incentives matter; have to persuade people to believe that something can work in practice even if it does not work in theory.

So state policy leadership faces a huge challenge when trying to change traditional arrangements in public education. It must be able to explain its strategy. Especially it must be able to deal with five objections the opposition will inevitably throw up.

Five objections . . . with responses

Ideas matter because policymaking depends on the way people define problems and shape strategies. Those defending the status quo will try hard to steer the discussion toward what is not really the problem or toward some action they find non-threatening. The discussion about K-12 policy is filled with this struggle over how to set the questions.

Five assertions from the defenders of present arrangements are especially important.

- "Money makes the difference. What we really need is adequate financing."
- "Let's drop all this talk about structure and process. Let's get back to what's important, and focus on improving student learning."
- "Reform can't be just a single, isolated thing. There are no silver bullets. We have to act comprehensively, systemically, with all the changes aligned."
- "Be realistic: Most of the kids are in the district schools. That's where the job has got to be done."
- "What you're talking about would introduce choice, and choice will destroy public education."

1. There is no concept of 'adequate' financing

Only a little, really, needs to be said about the most common argument of all: that K-12 would be fine if the taxpayers and the legislature would just give the districts adequate financing.

The problem is that there is no concept of adequate—sufficient—financing. No definition of 'enough' will be accepted by the districts and their associations. So long as they feel they do not have the capacity to meet expectations for student learning the districts will hold on to the traditional defenses. And no defense has worked better than blaming 'inadequate resources'.

Beyond this, the unclarity about the objective to be reached creates uncertainty about 'how much'. The desire not to limit improvement clearly implies a need for 'more'. And of course—quite independent of the objectives and what is necessary to meet them—'more' is essential for the biennial salary increase.

So those in K-12 are likely always to be pressing for more; writing budgets that have to be 'cut' and then blaming the legislature for not providing 'enough'. The institution is absolutely addicted to this strategy. Some people close to the Minnesota debate remember a K-12 lobbyist answering the question "How much?" by saying: "All you've got plus 10 percent."

The financing arrangements are in fact structured to drive expenditure. Those in K-12 fight hard to keep open the right for wealthy districts to go beyond what the state provides. These are described as 'lighthouse' districts, striving for quality. Soon rich districts are spending significantly more per pupil. Then a cry goes up that this is inequitable. Lawsuits are filed. Bills are introduced to reduce the disparity. Money is provided to bring the low-spending districts up. But no one closes off that opportunity for high-value districts to go beyond. So the process begins again, the disparity stretching out and closing up over time like a caterpillar moving along a porch railing.

The discussion about adequacy needs to be shifted away from money, to focus on the (in)adequacy of the system arrangements. A skillful governor could do this. Next time a suit is filed, alleging the state is failing to provide a 'thorough and efficient' (an adequate) system of education, resist the attorney general's instinctive impulse to deny the complaint. Admit the complaint; not with respect to money but with respect to the system arrangements. Argue that 'efficient' means what the dictionary says: capable of accomplishing the result intended. Show that as presently arranged K-12 is incapable of accomplishing the result intended. Make the system-arrangements the issue in adequacy. Otherwise the question will always be framed in money terms and, with no one to explain why money alone does not create the capacity to improve, a court accepting the need for improvement will almost certainly order an increase in spending.[1]

2. Goals are important, but success requires a method

A surprising number of people want to talk just about goals, about the good things that need to be done. They do not want to talk about method, about how to get it done.

Some issues are of course about objectives. But agreement on the objective forces the question of method. The legislator will ask, "What do you want me to do?" You cannot say, "Improve teaching": Legislators cannot enact 'better teaching'. You have to talk to legislators in terms of doing what will result in better teaching. There has to be a method, a means, a strategy. The issue is always method: What will actually work and what will not? People who only re-state the objectives are a distraction from real solutions.

People will disagree about method. Some will favor commands and regulations. Some will favor incentives. Some will think the strategy should be to spend more and to get better leadership; some will disagree with that. Some will argue simply for fixing the schools we have; others will want also to create good schools new. Some will favor national action; some state and local action. Getting agreement will take time.

---

[1] In Kentucky state leadership did cooperate in a lawsuit that asserted inadequacy beyond just financing.

The current discussion is not enough about method. Too much is still about objectives. Over and over, as often in 'Commentary' on the back page of *Education Week*, administrators and professors urge us all to get back to what's really important. Kids should be able to read well, teachers should teach well, all students should meet high standards. Too much of the discussion that follows simply exhorts people to do good things; says that boards and administrators and teachers should do this and should do that, must do this and must do that. Where does that take us?

There has to be a method, some—valid—theory of action. In a real sense the method is the solution.

Hope is not a method

It is not helpful to put forward a method that cannot realistically be implemented. "Give me $50 million and get the union off my back and I can do this job", I heard a superintendent in Ohio say once. When you hear a 'strategy' proposed, listen for, probe for, the often-unstated conditions that need to be met for it to succeed. A solution that cannot be implemented is not a solution.

Looking back at it later, an evaluation identified the assumptions underlying the Children Achieving initiative in Philadelphia. The success of the superintendent's initiative depended, it said, on political backing from the mayor, on support from the business community, on financing from the state and on cooperation from the union. Clearly it was critical whether those conditions could be assumed. In Philadelphia, as it turned out, they could not be.

Missionaries—dedicated, earnest and persuasive—hope that believers will follow, thus fulfilling what has been promised. And sometimes people do follow: People want to believe a person presumed to know. But hope is a dangerous strategy. You can say that given following winds of no more than 10 miles an hour and seas no higher than three feet and regular deliveries of food and water you can sail your 25-foot boat from New York to London. And given those conditions you probably could. You could set out hoping for those conditions. But that means nothing. Those conditions cannot be assumed.

Such 'hoping' is what Warren Buffett calls "the Tinker Bell" approach: that fairies live if people believe in them. Into 2000 some people were saying they believed the stock market could return 12 percent or more a year. Buffett had challenged that. A realistic estimate of economic growth and interest rates, looking forward, suggested six or seven percent on the average, the chairman of Berkshire Hathaway said in the November 1999 issue of Fortune. "Now maybe you'd like to argue a different case. Fair enough. But give me your assumptions. I think you have to say, for example, 'I expect GDP to grow at 10 percent a year, dividends to add two percentage points to returns and interest rates to stay at a constant level'. Or you've got to rearrange these variables in some other manner." This is a fair test to set for those advocating this or that strategy for improving education: Give us your assumptions; prove they are valid.

The states are beginning to realize that the strategy since the mid-1980s—trying to drive change in existing schools within existing arrangements with regulations linked to federal aid—has relied too much on hope and on assumptions that might not hold. They cannot afford this risk. They are beginning now to develop a strategy, a method, that relies not only on making improvement necessary for the districts in their own interest but also on ensuring there will be different and better schools created whether the districts act or not.

3. 'Systemic' need not mean 'comprehensive'

Another serious complication in the policy discussion arises, ironically, from those proponents who insist that change must be 'comprehensive'. From those who say that policy must deal with standards and curriculum and instruction and testing and consequences and finance and teacher-training and perhaps even with governance all together. This is one notion of 'systemic change': all actions aligned, in an intricate process of master planning.

The real world of policymaking cannot handle the complexity this involves. Legislators are paralyzed by these elaborate schemes with their long timetables for staged implementation.

Experienced, realistic legislators know it is not practical to be so comprehensive. To identify all the implications and to require policymakers to bring them through the processes of politics would in fact frustrate change. It is beyond the capacity of the political process to design-in all the elements of a new arrangement, to make explicit all the second-order consequences of all the changes involved, and to try to put all of the implications to a vote. To do that would multiply the opposition's ability to spread fear and doubt and would ensure failure. Talk of 10-year implementation assumes a continuity in political institutions that does not exist.

For these reasons the 'comprehensive' change, the engineered solutions favored by some consultants and policy thinkers, is another method that is probably not realistically a solution and is unlikely to be effective.

Legislators do think systemically and do act systemically. Over time they change institutions and systems dramatically. But they use a more strategic concept of 'systemic' that is different from the notion of acting comprehensively.

Changing just a single 'part' is systemic change!

Think back to Chapter 1 and its discussion about the two meanings of 'system'. One defines a system in terms of its parts; in K-12, the organizations that make up what we are calling here the institution. The other looks at what we have called the rules of the game, the principles that govern the organizations' behavior.

It really is possible sometimes to produce change by altering one part of (or introducing one new part into) the institution, or by altering just one of the rules of the game. It is not essential to act comprehensively in order to produce a general, even radical, change. A single discrete action can generate dynamics that ripple through the institution over time, so that as other parts respond and adapt the whole gradually changes.

Consider telecommunications. As microwave towers and the communications satellite appeared, the old industry based on 'long lines' changed dramatically. New competitors went after just the long-distance traffic. "They are driving us out of the price-averaging business", I heard the chief engineer of Northwestern Bell Telephone Co. say in the 1970s. The old parts of the institution at first tried to resist. But then the CEO of AT&T decided to embrace deregulation and competition. Service changed, products changed, prices changed. Telecommunications has been transformed, and change continues to sweep through the industry.

Consider cities. The arrival of the railroads sent old river towns into decline and caused other cities to grow. The introduction of the automobile and the motor truck into cities built in the streetcar era created a new and different (sub)urban pattern, spreading and decentralizing residential and commercial development; moving homes and businesses, setting off related changes in life styles, culture, politics and governance. Transportation and land use are interacting parts of the urban system: The automobile creates low densities that can be served only by the automobile. Rail transit requires high-density development: If we want to travel like Europeans we cannot live like Americans.

Transformations of this sort were not comprehensive, preplanned and managed with all actions aligned. Most large-scale change is like this: a new dynamic introduced into 'a collection of interacting parts'; change spreading gradually as existing elements adapt.

The difference between the two notions of systemic change is pretty much Professor Charles Lindblom's distinction between "mechanisms of central authority" and "mechanisms of mutual adjustment". There is an intellectual conception of comprehensive action, Lindblom argued, but in reality most social action proceeds in a process of "disjointed incrementalism". The influence of people trained to think in terms of the situation in its entirety, with their bias in favor of acting comprehensively, "continues to be one of the major intellectual problems in the organization of human action", he said in 1987 in a talk at the University of Minnesota.[2]

---

[2]See also his *The Intelligence of Democracy*, Basic Books, New York, 1965 and *Politics and Markets*, The Free Press, New York, 1977.

Find 'the one thing that leads on to everything else'

Policy leadership, then, might be much better advised to follow the strategy that Richard Murnane and Frank Levy advocate, picking up on Albert Hirschman's insight about the best approach to economic development. That was to "start with the initiative that creates the most pressure for other constructive changes". Previously in that field the notion had been balanced growth, moving on all fronts at once. This sounded wonderful, Murnane and Levy write, but required an effort at coordination well beyond the capability of most governments.[3]

Jean Monnet and his colleagues, in 1950, knew that the integration of the old system of European nation-states could not be brought about in a single stroke. For him the question was where to begin. Everything is possible, he wrote, once you find "the one precise point that leads on to everything else". The decision was to begin with the limited delegation of sovereignty that pooled the iron and steel industries of Germany and France. Over time other countries and other sectors followed. Francois Duchene wrote in his biography that "Monnet and his entourage used to talk in the early days of 'dynamic disequilibrium'. All this really meant at first was that the Coal and Steel Community was not viable on its own in the long run and so would create tensions with national processes which would become unmanageable unless there was progress to new communities. The assertion was vague and the possibility of an unwinding of the Community was ignored. There have been times when one could wonder whether the dynamic was real. But after 40 years it seems the intuition was fundamentally correct."[4]

Some might ask: Is it possible that the introduction of standards and measurement represents that discrete change in the system, that "one precise point that leads on to everything else"?

Perhaps. But probably not. This notion of systemic change implies and requires an open institution, in which the other parts are both motivated and able to respond. This returns us to our original question about the capacity of K-12 to change. And to the willingness of the district sector to accept accountability as a 'have to'. The problem is that the consequences of not-complying are at this point not really very serious. If tagged as 'failing' a district is likely to have a good deal of company. At worst it will be told to give some students the opportunity to transfer or to get additional tutoring.

More likely the one action that leads on to everything else in K-12 education is the action to withdraw the district's exclusive; to pull out the traditional given that

---

[3]See *Teaching the New Basic Skills*, The Free Press, 1996. Murnane is a professor in Harvard's Graduate School of Education, Levy a professor of urban economics at MIT.

[4]*Jean Monnet, First Statesman of Interdependence*, W.W. Norton, 1994.

has had this institution arranged in a public-utility model. This is not the prevailing theory of systemic reform, which is emphatic about moving within the public-utility framework of traditional public education and on all fronts at once. But it is systemic change and it is increasingly the emerging second dimension of state strategy.

No silver bullets' and "We're not ready"

The concept of creating dynamic disequilibrium, of using a discrete adjustment in the institution or a change in the rules of the game to drive change through the institution, puts into perspective two other objections commonly thrown up by those resisting change.

Apologists for the status quo will often use the old saw about there being "no silver bullets" to try to knock down proposals designed to trigger a change they see would disrupt the institution. This is a simplistic version of the argument that all action must be comprehensive, suggesting that no single action can possibly be sufficient. Yet as the examples make clear, changing just a single 'part' can often set in motion a process of system change. At the heart of complexities, Monnet wrote, things are simple.

Clearly, a single, discrete action is the logical action where only one essential element is missing. As K-12 is now arranged incentives are missing. Those trying to introduce these incentives are not suggesting this is the only action needed. They understand the need also for standards, measurement and consequences, for better leadership and for adequate financing. They are simply pointing out that incentives are missing and that unless there are incentives public education will not become a self-improving institution.

Those resisting change will also try to get us to believe that people must be trained before anything new can be introduced. This appears in the education debate as the notion that decisions cannot be decentralized until those in the school have been taught to manage well. Or that choice cannot be introduced until parents have been trained to choose well.

Again: This is not the way the world works. Change almost always happens before everything is ready. Nobody said that we couldn't let people sell cars until everybody knew how to drive or until enough roads had been built. When the need appears, people act. Before the need is real few reasonable people would bother.[5]

'Disjointed incrementalism' is unsettling. Things seem out of control. People fear that bad things might happen (meaning, presumably, would not happen if we

---

[5]Training may not be essential. In central Harlem in the early 1980s enrollment was rising at two of the junior high schools, dropping at the other. These decisions, largely by welfare mothers, "coincided perfectly with my professional judgment about the respective merits of the three schools involved", the administrator of that New York City community district said at a meeting in 1984.

acted comprehensively). But as change proceeds the course can be corrected with other adjustments in the system. So there is a concept of public management of the process as a whole.

Superintendents sometimes object that setting in motion this kind of fundamental change is like asking them "to remodel the airplane while still flying it", as if that were manifestly absurd. But of course changing on the fly is what most organizations have to do. Ask the CEO of a telecommunications company or of a financial institution—or, these days, of an insurance business or computer business. No one in these industries gets to shut down while the firm converts to a new technology or new business model.

4. Go *where the most progress is possible*

The defenders of existing arrangements counter the argument for new schools by saying what they feel is unarguable. Most of the kids are in the district schools. So to improve education for most kids we have to improve the district schools. That's what we're trying to do, they say. Don't get caught up in choice and new schools. That's peripheral, a diversion from the real task. Help us to change.

This clearly has a major effect on key people the mainline groups count on for support: much of the business community, some foundations, often the media and elected officials. It seems so logical. It seems realistic.

Hidden inside this, of course, is the assumption that the districts can improve the schools they have. This assumption is usually not explicit. But it is the foundation on which rests the argument for focusing only on the districts. The assumption is that the districts can change enough, and quickly enough, to get their schools to educate all kids to high standards.

Yet this may not be so. Think back to Clayton Christensen's analysis of the (in)capacity of private organizations to change. If business corporations cannot significantly change why would a reasonable person believe change will be easier, even possible, for organizations in the public and political sector?

I think about a teacher I know in Minneapolis. He was closely involved some years back with one of the district's alternative schools. He wrote a wonderful paper at that time, explaining the things that need to be done differently in order to succeed with at-risk students. Schools had to be small; perhaps no more than 80 students. Every adult must teach. The curriculum must be broken down into something like eight-week blocks. These kids live turbulent lives, and family problems can easily take them out of school for two weeks. Students who fail a semester are likely to fall seriously behind, and students who fail two are likely not to graduate. Eight-week blocks mean that if a student misses two weeks s/he will not fail a semester. And so forth.

This teacher is now back in a mainline high school. When I talked to him recently he was struggling with its difficulties. I took him back to what he had learned in that alternative school. It was clear this had no meaning for him now. It is not possible to make his current school work on those principles. He has to do what he can in that 2,000-student school, has to accept that it really cannot change.

State policy leadership will have to continue to do what it can to help the districts improve their schools. But it is unrealistic to expect the incremental improvements that are possible to make very much difference very quickly. State strategy will need to move beyond this, with a much more aggressive effort to create schools new. For the community, for the state and for the country the process of improvement is a process of replacing, gradually, old schools with new schools, different schools.

Governors and legislators will need to be firm: Some students do want quite radically different schools. Some will learn only in a radically different school: They are failing in regular school and incremental improvements on the old model offer nothing to them. Some others want to move faster and at their own pace through the curriculum. With both kinds of students it is not enough just to hope it will prove possible to transform existing schools.

Those concerned with change usually suggest the burden of proof is on ideas that have not been tried. Not today. Today, after decades of tinkering with the old model of education and the old methods of improvement, the burden of proof is on the ideas that have been tried.

5. Public education is a 'choice' system today

One of the most contentious questions in the discussion about changing public education's system arrangements has been the question of choice.

As policymakers withdraw the old rules—that you were assigned to school where you lived and that where you lived there was only one organization offering public education—people get the impression that choice is just now being introduced. They worry what will happen and express their concern about "the kids who will be left behind". Surely, they say, this proposed change gives reason for concern.

Nothing could be further from the truth.

Choice exists

Public education is a choice arrangement today. It has been at least since the *Pierce* decision in the 1920s. People really do choose the schools they want their children to attend. And this is true not only of those using private schools. Choice is a central element of public education, of the district arrangement.

It is right to be concerned about the equity effects of choice. But we need to understand: We are today at the end of a long period of sorting-out, with millions of children left behind by the deeply inequitable institution that public education has become.

We all know how metropolitan areas are built, with houses of like value grouped together. We understand the relationship between house value and family income. We know the demographics of family income. When we set down over an urban region built like this a grid of picket-fences called school-district-boundaries, requiring kids to attend school in the district in which they live, we create an institution stratified by income, social class and race. This fairly describes what exists today in the metropolitan regions where three-quarters of the people live. John Coons, the law professor who wrote the brief in the California *Serrano* case, likes to say, "A Marxist could have a field day with the American public education system".

The Governor's Discussion Group in Minnesota got quickly to this reality one afternoon in late 1985. Set up by Gov. Rudy Perpich, the group consisted of the elected heads and staff directors of the big education associations and a roughly equal number of persons involved with Perpich in his open-enrollment initiative in the legislative session that year. Robert Astrup, then president of the Minnesota Education Association, started off with the "I'm concerned . . ." speech. Verne Johnson challenged him.

"Bob, choice exists", Johnson said. "Nobody has to send their kids to school anywhere. You can enroll your kids wherever you want. You can choose the district you want; you can go to private school. It does take money. But if you have money you have choice. Lots of people choose; everywhere, all the time. Those without money can't. Some of us are trying to use public resources to offset those inequalities in private resources. That sounds to us like a liberal thing to do. Why are you against it?"

Coons, in Minneapolis in the early 1980s, had made the same point. "It was clear to me that some people had choice and some did not; and that this difference was related to wealth. I felt we should standardize on one principle or the other: Either everybody should have the right to choose, or nobody should have it. As a liberal democrat I come down in favor of everybody having it."

It is a disturbing question why those arguing so intensely against choice are so reluctant to acknowledge the choice plan in operation today; why they so often talk as if what is out there is literally the common school of our theory. It is hard to believe they do not see what exists. If their concern is genuine you would expect them to be protesting the inequity that affects so many children now. The disturbing possibility is that they do see it—and prefer not to talk about it.

The failure to talk realistically about public education as a choice arrangement today, the tendency to talk as if choice is only now being introduced, is seriously confusing our national discussion. We need to start with the fact that choice exists, and then talk sensibly about how the current inequity can be relieved.

The issue is a practical question, of design

To have an intelligent discussion about choice we need to get to specifics. It is unhelpful to talk in the abstract. Choice is different from assignment, and that difference is important. But legislators cannot write laws simply substituting choice for assignment. They have to work with specific plans.

Think again about riding, which surely is different than walking. You would not go into a showroom and ask the salesman to sell you something to ride in. The dealer will want you to be specific; to talk about a sedan or a pickup or a convertible or a motorcycle or a truck or whatever. Nothing can happen until you get beyond the abstraction of riding.

It's the same with choice. Choice in the abstract is for ideologues. Practical people have to talk about specific plans. The equity effects and quality effects all depend on the way legislators answer three key questions: What students will be eligible to choose? What schools will be available for them to attend? Under what rules do the students and the schools come together?

For each of these questions there are several possible answers.

■ *Which students will be eligible to choose?*

It could be all students. Or just certain students; low-income students perhaps. Or perhaps students not doing well. Or just students who fall into certain defined categories, as under Minnesota's High School Graduation Incentives legislation: parent, pregnant, behind in age level, behind in grade level, adjudicated, chronically truant. Or it could be just students in certain locations: in big cities, for example, or in failing schools.

Traditionally the criterion for choice has been whether a student's parents can afford it. We can do better than that.

■ *What schools may the students choose to attend?*

It might be only the schools of the district in which the student lives: This is intra-district choice. Or the plan might include the schools of other districts, as under a typical plan for inter-district open enrollment. Or a plan might include colleges and universities, as under Minnesota's Post-secondary Enrollment Options program. The choices might extend to schools created new by teachers and others as under the chartering laws.

A plan might make available schools existing or newly created in the private-education sector. This is now the meaning of 'vouchers'. Such a plan, in turn, might or might not include religious schools. That has been an important issue in the design of the voucher programs in Milwaukee and Cleveland.

Or students might be able to choose to study independently—which might or might not mean literally at home—with graduation validated by success on the assessment.

■ *Under what rules will student and school come together?*

It will need to be clear, first, on what basis students will be admitted. May the school select its students? If so, on what basis? May prior academic record and disciplinary record be considered, or not? If the school specializes in a particular field, may applicants be required to demonstrate interest and experience in that field? If the school cannot select its students then will it have a first-come, first-served arrangement or will every student have an equal chance of being admitted through a random draw? Will there be racial preferences or quotas? Will non-discrimination laws apply?

Will the school be free to the student, or not? If tuition is charged, will the state payment cover all the cost or only part of the cost? Will there be scholarships for economically needy students? If so, on what basis will these be granted? Whatever the level of revenue made available, will the school or admitting district be required to accept that payment and to enroll that student?

On and on. The answers to the questions define the plan. Decisions need to be made. Then the answers need to be widely known. Somebody has to make that information available.

One conceivable plan would answer: all kids, any local district, and only if the family can afford to buy a house within that district. This is basically the plan we call 'public education' today. Another might be: all kids, all schools, including private and religious, and under the rules that private schools use today, with fees charged and selective admission.

Neither of these is an equitable plan, and neither is the inevitable working of the choice idea. They are simply particular designs that happen to be in use or proposed. Other and more equitable plans are possible. The discussion about equity has to be in terms of the specific plan in use or proposed. Occasionally an academic or theorist will study one of the badly-designed and clearly inequitable plans and then write a book announcing that 'choice' has failed. In truth a badly-designed plan has failed. So: Design a better, a fairer, plan.

A plan to improve on the inequitable arrangement in public education today might offer choice to kids now disadvantaged in their present schools, might make available both district and non-district schools and might adopt the rules of public education: no charging tuition, no teaching religion, no picking and choosing nice kids. This is essentially the public-school choice design appearing in some states. Much the same rules are built into the charter idea.

The voucher debate is now about the schools to be available

The voucher discussion today is no longer essentially about choice.

It was, into the 1980s, before the 'exclusive' began to be withdrawn in public education and when students were still assigned to school. That changed as state policy leadership began to make it possible for students to enroll in schools in other districts. Students could decide where to enroll and public money would follow. This extended choice within public education. In the 1990s the chartered schools became part of the state's program of public education, adding still more public schools of choice.

Today, with the principle of choice established within public education, the non-public school is simply another of the possible choic/es. The remaining question, the residual meaning of 'voucher', is whether legislation should open up private education as another new organizational space in which people can create and run schools that students may choose to attend with public money following.

Different states make somewhat different decisions. Minnesota's plan is a public strategy without private schools, containing inter-district open enrollment, an option for 11th- and 12th-graders to finish high school in college, and chartered schools. Wisconsin, for Milwaukee, its one big urban district, uses mostly a combination of chartered schools and vouchers. Its voucher program first excluded religious schools, later was modified to include them.

The issue comes to focus in the cities

Over the years the choice program that depends on private family wealth—families choosing where they want to live—has left millions of poor kids behind in the older central cities. It is here, with these kids, that the toughest issues arise.

After the protests and riots of the 1960s there was briefly some thought that policy might open an opportunity for the urban poor to live outside the central city. This was a theme in the report of the Kerner Commission in the late 1960s. If the concentrations of poor and minorities could be broken up, the thinking ran, dispersal might be acceptable to the largely white suburbs. But the suburbs did not agree. Nor did the political leaders of the rising minority-majority about to take control of City Hall and of the central-city board of education.

So, with residential segregation a reality, there came next an effort to transport the students from where they lived to where the good schools were, and to create racial balance through busing. Desegregation orders appeared in many cities and— sometimes against resistance that turned violent—accomplished some racial balance. But as the minority population grew within the city these plans accomplished less, and began to generate resistance among African-Americans whose children were disproportionately those being transported. Polly Williams, a state representative from Milwaukee, would throw photos of school-bus accidents on the screen, one after another. "Look at the faces," she said. "Whose children are these? Look at the faces."

It was never really possible to extend desegregation plans beyond the city limits. By the 1990s, with minority enrollment in the city schools rising past 50 percent toward 100 percent, more and more desegregation orders were withdrawn.

The effort now to give inner-city students access to quality is to create good schools where they live. Gleason Glover, then president of the Minneapolis Urban League, was pressed one noon in the mid-1980s by state department of education officials and others to endorse a desegregation program for the Twin Cities area. Glover declined to do that. He had grown up in Newport News, Va. "We didn't want to go to the white schools because they were white schools", he said. "We wanted to go to those schools because we perceived them as good schools. Just get us quality schools". That was all he would say.[6]

Concentrated in the older central areas, the poor had little choice. They depended on the local district to get them quality schools. The failure of these districts to deliver was a tragedy. It is this failure in central-city public education that has drawn the states into their most significant institutional changes: into takeover, into chartering, into experiments with contracting, into vouchers. All are efforts to open up choic/es where poor kids live. This is now increasingly the goal of the African-American leadership assembled by Howard Fuller as the Black Alliance for Educational Options (BAEO). The struggle for good schools is now seen by some as a new frontier of the civil-rights movement.

'They're taking our money!'

After "What about the kids who are left behind?" the most common attack that district officials make, as a choice program takes hold, is to say, "They're taking away our money". When a student moves out our district loses, at a minimum, our state aid for that child. Our expenses for heat, light, maybe even staffing don't go down. So we have to cut program or increase class size. Kids get hurt.

There are several things to say about this.

"We have a pupil-driven formula", state Rep. Becky Kelso told the administrators in Northfield, Minn., in one discussion about the chartering law. "You have more students, the state sends you more money. You have fewer, we send less. Enrollment goes up, enrollment goes down. It happens. You're a manager; you adjust". Besides,

---

[6]In the spring of 2004 black parents in Boston were saying exactly this. We asked for quality schools and you gave us busing. We asked for quality schools again and you gave us 'assignment zones'. Give us quality schools. *Boston Globe*, April 8, 2004.

she said, when 10 new students arrive your costs for heat, light and perhaps even staffing don't go up either, but your revenue goes up by the full per-pupil amount.[7]

The district response perfectly illustrates the assumption that the way of doing things cannot change: We can do more, we can do less, we cannot do different. So revenue changes are allowed to play out as negative impacts on students. Adults are not to be hurt: There is little thought, for example, that the salary increase would be held down to make revenue available to maintain program or class size.[8]

Enrollment may drop for all kinds of reasons, student choice but one of them. The state cannot afford to protect districts from the financial consequences of demographic change. Nor should it protect a district from decisions by parents seeking better schooling than they believe that district provides.

Is 'saving the district' the most important goal?

A Minneapolis school board member with whom I occasionally talk argues earnestly the overriding importance of preserving the district.

He argues that it is through this mechanism that the community decides how to educate its children, decides what they should know and who should teach them and how much it should spend. If the schools are not all district schools, if various organizations are responsible for schools and if parents choose, then—he tells me—the public character of education and the values of community are lost. It is an argument that appears in the national discussion as the insistence that accountability must be 'democratic accountability'; direct control of all schools through the board elected by the voters.

Not everyone accepts the notion that we find our community through politics; the notion of "the larger community, represented by government" (as I heard a professor at the Harvard Graduate School of Education put it once). Many believe that civil society is larger than government; that if the current arrangements set up in government do not put student interests first then the people can act to change these arrangements.

This discussion is partly about the difference between the way the idea of 'the district' works in theory and the way it works in reality. Gradually attitudes are becoming more realistic. In a discussion after a dinner at the Brookings Institution one evening in 1997 Professor James Comer expressed his concern about the effect

---

[7]Minnesota treats the marginal student as fully state-paid, so moves the full education-revenue amount when a student enrolls or leaves.

[8]In fact, salary settlements often require cuts in program and in staffing where there is no enrollment change. In the late 1980s I mentioned the new contract in the Mounds View district to a vice president of the Minnesota Education Association. "That settlement will cost jobs", he said. In Forest Lake, Minn., in June 1991 the union itself proposed sacrificing 31 teacher jobs to generate revenue for the salary increase.

that a choice plan, if introduced, might have on 'the system'. Mayor Kurt Schmoke quickly invited him to come with him to the west side of Baltimore to explain to 'Mrs. Smith' that she shouldn't be able to transfer her son to a better school because that might have a bad effect on 'the system'. That uncomfortable moment ended the discussion.

John Gardner, formerly the at-large member on the Milwaukee board, is not so gentle with the middle-class people who worry about the effect on 'the system'. "You would never let them put your child in some of the schools we've got," he will say when he hears the "I'm concerned . . ." speech. "You would move, you would pay tuition, you would go to work to earn the money, you would do anything to keep that from happening. How dare you tell people who haven't got the resources you've got that they can't have the opportunity you have, to do what they think is best for their children? How dare you?"

The assertion that the processes of government are morally superior to choice is stunningly insensitive to the way the political process compounds the present social inequity. In Albert Hirschman's terms: Those with money, who have an advantage in exit, have also the advantage in voice. Their education, their experience, their political skills and their influence both with elected officials and with administrators gives them an advantage with the board, with the central office and with the principal and teachers in the school. It is disappointing, but perhaps not surprising, to find those with this advantage in voice arguing against choice, insisting on the process of politics. A cynic would say it is no accident.

In the current process, dominated by voice and in which exit depends on private wealth, the poor are doubly disadvantaged. Choice on the other hand—the opportunity "to leave and to take my money with me"—has the potential to put the poor on something like an even footing.

PART FOUR

HOW QUICKLY CAN IT BE DONE?

Chapter 12

IF THE LEADERSHIP IN K-12 DECIDES TO MOVE . . .

State policy leadership has the power to turn public education into a self-improving institution. But how quickly the governors and legislators can act will be heavily affected by the decision of those inside the K-12 institution.

Superintendents, boards, teachers and their state and national associations can decide to support or to oppose the states' effort to change the K-12 system. They can speed up or slow down the progress of the change. They can decide to create new schools or can decline to create new schools. It is becoming an urgent question which way the leadership will go. The question has both practical and ethical dimensions.

Agreed solutions are always easier than imposed solutions. Change will be harder if the district institution resists. Resistance will force a conflict that will be contentious, painful, and time-consuming. It would be immensely helpful if those inside the institution would acknowledge the ineffectiveness of the effort simply to transform existing schools; if someone somewhere in this K-12 institution would emerge to say: We have been trying to do what cannot work. We have got to stop this. Even if it calls our traditions into question, we have got to do what can work.[1]

The states' initiative is already testing boards, administrators and unions. The question sits in front of them at the national, state and local level: How are we going to respond to the pressure for change?

In private conversations there is often some sense that the pressures are causing thoughtful insiders to think about the need to move.[2] This could create a real

---

[1] I remember talking once with the manager of the transit system in the Kansas City area. He had cooperated with the effort of a suburban community, Blue Springs, to opt out of the transit district. The manager acknowledged: This is heresy in the transit business, where everybody is supposed to be part of a single service district. But these people can clearly get more service than I can give them, by moving on their own. How can I justify standing in their way?

[2] At the start of the Governor's Discussion Group in Minnesota in 1985 someone suggested the group not argue about what's past. "I'm glad to hear you say that," Willard Baker, the executive of the school boards association responded. "We'll stipulate: We can do better."

opportunity for state policy leadership to act. Improvement might then move rapidly. But it is also possible that those inside will be unwilling to break publicly with the old theology of public education. They may decide instead to continue the classic plea for more time, more support and more resources, even as the citizenry and state policy leadership continue to lose confidence in the old public-utility model.

There are reasons to be hopeful that the K-12 leadership will put the public interest ahead of the institutional interest. Equally, there are reasons not to be hopeful.

Sometimes leadership does move

In some institutions approaching crisis leadership has emerged, acknowledging reality and taking the risk involved in change.

Consider, for example, the leadership of the organization then known as the American Association of State Highway Officials (AASHO).

Planning for what became the Interstate highway program began in the 1940s, following the Bureau of Public Roads' report "Interregional Highways" in 1944. The new freeways were to provide transportation within as well as between the nation's big metropolitan areas. Designing and building these freeways was a new job for organizations that had grown up after about 1916 building roads in rural areas. The typical highway department had little experience building in cities. This inexperience, and the engineers' insensitivity to the impact of their roads on neighborhoods, led to some serious mistakes in routing and in design. Quickly controversies appeared. Even by 1956 serious resistance was developing, from the rising profession of city planning and from the media—all visible in the Hartford Conference that year.

Alf Johnson, then executive director of AASHO, embarked on a major effort to persuade the state roadbuilding establishment that in cutting these major roads through cities it had to adapt its attitudes and its procedures. This was not welcomed by the old-line engineers. But month after month into the 1960s, in state after state, Johnson was at their meetings, pounding away with his message: If we do not change, route-planning and road design will be taken away from us. Gradually practices did change, as old attitudes softened and as traditional people were replaced. It was a remarkable case of leadership; an association executive challenging the core traditions of his member-organizations.

Some similar initiatives appear in local government. While executive secretary of the League of Municipalities in Minnesota in the 1940s Orville Peterson could see that the population bottled up in the old housing stock in Minneapolis and Saint Paul during World War II was about to spill out into new subdivisions beyond the borders of the cities. Out there was suburban 'village' government, virtually without professional staff, totally unprepared for what was coming. In 1947 Peterson persuaded the Legislature to put into law a process by which the suburban villages—among his association's members—could be converted to a manager form by public vote. Not all the local officials were happy. Not all the suburban residents were enthusiastic about growth. But the League pushed the program. The law got competent front-line local government into place just ahead of the wave of suburban development, just in time.

Might the K-12 leadership lead as well?

Between 1987 and 1992 Albert Shanker went about as far as a president of the American Federation of Teachers could go to set out the problem and to suggest what needed to be done. When *A Nation at Risk* appeared he immediately urged his membership not to resist its criticisms. Rather, he said, let's acknowledge its truth, then turn it to our advantage. From his efforts came the Carnegie Forum rebuttal, *A Nation Prepared*, urging the professionalization of teaching.

Shanker's willingness to challenge the conventional rhetoric of union policy is reflected in an obscure volume of 'recollections' assembled by Phi Delta Kappa in 1991. Part of it is worth quoting.

> For 20 years the union's agenda was to increase salaries and reduce class size. . . This program was widely accepted by school boards, parents and communities as a strategy for school improvement. But by the early 1980s it was clear that carrying out the program would call for an amount of money and a level of staffing that realistically we could not expect to get.

> Bringing the average teacher's salary to $45,000 a year would mean an increase of $10,000 to $15,000 per teacher. Multiply this by 2.5 million teachers and it comes to something in the neighborhood of $30 billion a year more than what the country currently spends. And this is before adding in the cost of benefits.

> Decreasing class size . . . runs up against the same arithmetic. If we were to cut class size by one-third . . . we would need another 800,000 teachers. This represents an enormous amount of money, even with salaries at current levels. And we would not be able to find qualified people to fill the jobs anyway. We don't have a host of well-qualified candidates standing in line to be teachers. In fact, we already have some people in the classroom who are at the borderline of literacy and numeracy. Hiring more would mean digging deeper into the talent pool.

> The arithmetic . . . suggests we need to . . . find some other ways to accomplish these goals. We could change the way teachers teach, we could change the structure of schools and the structure of the teaching profession. If all the people working

in hospitals had to be doctors we would have seven million doctors rather than 500,000—and they would all be paid like teachers. There would be too many to educate as rigorously as we do now, so the standards of medical practice would probably be much lower than they are.

Shanker pointed policy toward differentiated staffing, toward the individualization of learning for students through technology, toward project-based learning (drawing from his experience in the Boy Scouts), toward performance-based assessment and toward the need for incentives, extrinsic as well as intrinsic, as a driver for change.

And, he said: "We do not have much time. . . If we are not able to produce— and quickly—a credible plan for moving school reform we may have reached the end of public education."[3]

Some leader, somewhere in the institution, could return now to the idea of changing the strategy, of changing the basic arrangements. When they decide something should happen the associations in K-12 are very skillful at moving an initiative. All of a sudden that topic is visible everywhere: newspapers are writing about it, conferences are being called to discuss it, foundations are making grants to expand it, legislators are being urged to finance it. What the leadership wants to get behind and push, does move.

This asks a lot. Still, those inside the institution do not actually have to get out front advocating the changes. Others will carry the advocacy. It would be enough for the leadership in K-12 just not to fight it, just to let it happen.

The discouraging thing is that even this might ask too much.

Why 'the leadership' might not move

It is very tough for boards and superintendents to challenge the core traditions of public education. The institution has been fixed in its present pattern for a long time. Its major associations have defended these arrangements. The conviction that the board's job is "to run the schools" reflects the commitment to the traditional public-utility arrangement. Some may say it is all right to change the institution, that "the church is not the faith". But this is not the way it looks to those inside the monasteries.

The impulse of the state associations, and arguably their job, is to defend the existing order of things. It asks a lot of the leaders of these associations to give up the theology, the belief-system on which their entire career has rested.

---

[3]*Reflections: Personal Essays by 33 Distinguished Educators*, Phi Delta Kappa Educational Foundation, Bloomington, Ind., 1991.

And it would be hard politically. These are consensus organizations. Their executives have to think about how fast the membership is ready to move. A strong executive may be willing to push the laggards, but s/he cannot move too far or too fast. And public policy is not, anyway, their primary charge. Though their members work in the public sector these are private organizations. They exist partly to serve their members' private interests: removing the caps on superintendents' salaries, protecting teacher-certification and seniority, lobbying for increased appropriations that can be turned into salary increases at bargaining time, protecting what boards see as their management rights. All these are legitimate interests, which the associations are entitled to defend. But they are essentially private interests.

A few key attitudes and system-features drive this resistance.

■ *'Schools we don't run are not our schools'*

The president of the National School Boards Association told *Education Week* at the time Anne Bryant was appointed that it was good to have a strong new executive director because, he said, "We're the ones who run the schools". This view of the board "running the schools" makes the district institution deeply hostile to the idea that its role should be to assemble—on charter and on contract—the best possible collection of learning opportunities for the children of the community.

Site-management, contracting and chartering conflict with the culture of the K-12 institution. The district's whole tradition is to own and run almost everything it does. It operates a buildings-and-grounds business, an accounting business, a food-service business, a transportation business and often a security business.[4]

It is especially hard for district officials to contemplate not running the learning business. Running the schools is its business; is what it does, is what the district is. To have schools run by others seems to superintendents an admission of failure. A good manager should be able to run good schools. "Someone else is saying they can run a school better than I can, and I resent that," one Minnesota superintendent said about the chartering idea. Another wrote: "Chartering is a problem, because in some ways, districts might have to admit that there may be a better way to do education than the way they are doing it presently. It takes a pretty big person to be comfortable enough with who they are or stable enough in their position to be able to do that".

The problem with that attitude is obvious. But there it is.

At a minimum, as Randy Quinn pointed out, chartering changes the district's

---

[4]I heard the executive of the California School Boards Association say once that Los Angeles Unified runs the second largest law-enforcement organization in the state of California. Grievances from these employees must come to the board, he said.

role.[5] The district today controls through ownership and management, by having its hands on process and on personnel. When a school does not work the superintendent sends in a new principal. A chartered school that does not work must be closed. Control through performance raises difficult issues. If a board closed a chartered school that did not perform, would it be equally willing to close an owned school that did not perform?

Even if we were to accept what most of those on boards of education say, about being devoted to educating kids, we have to see that they are caught in the role the institutional arrangement provides them. They sit both as the board of the operating company and as the policy body for local public education. At election time members tell the parents and voters they mean to get the best possible education for the children. When elected they do nothing of the kind: They put the kids into the schools of the learning corporation in which they serve as the officers and directors. It is an act of self-dealing.

In the fall of 1999 a commission on governance set up by the Education Commission of the States suggested districts might consider putting *all* their schools into chartered status, creating an all-charter district.[6] This challenged the culture directly, and the National School Boards Association resisted. The NSBA opposition did not stop the commission's recommendations: ECS formed a Center on Governance and is continuing to work on the charter-district idea. Progress, however, is slow.

The decisions and the controversies involved in starting new schools may also just be more than the board can handle politically, more than the superintendent wants to handle politically. For most boards and superintendents life is incremental change. To be starting new schools and closing old ones, to be managing contracts rather than people, not to have your hands on the schools, not to be directly in control: It is all so very different.

Radical change—in the relationship of board and superintendent to the school and in the nature of the school—is just not on the agenda. District officials live with severe constraints on their ability to change. Boards block superintendents. Superintendents sometimes block boards. Both feel blocked by the unions, against which they usually claim to be helpless.

Incrementalism becomes the culture. Paul Houston, the executive of the American Association of School Administrators says simply: "If you are a superintendent you *are* in the 'incremental' business". After two years on the Saint Paul board Anne Carroll expressed the same conclusion: "It is not realistic to be radical". Reviewing

---

[5]See page 78.

[6]This idea should not be confused with some superintendents' idea of a district itself being on a charter from the state; the notion of a deregulated district.

New American Schools after its first decade RAND Corporation concluded that "Externally developed educational reform interventions cannot be 'break the mold' and still be marketable and implementable in current district and school contexts".[7]

The problem, of course, is that incremental change is not an effective response to the radical challenge now confronting the districts.

■ *Boards lack the capacity to lead*

Local policy leadership can sometimes be effective. In the mid-1960s, for example, when Minnesota was debating what to do about local government organization and finance in its big metropolitan area and was considering a radical change in the region's urban governmental arrangements, the lead was taken by the mayors in the League of Metropolitan Municipalities. Their commitment was extraordinary: In the year before the Legislature acted the mayor of Minnetonka, Al Illies, went to 263 meetings.

That debate was productive largely because those involved were elected officials, citizens serving part-time and for a few years who were charged to represent their cities but who were able also to think about the needs of the region in ways their professional managers could not. And the mayors in the end supported the creation of a new and directly-elected Metropolitan Council. This would never have been the result had the decision been in the hands of the managers, whose jobs, incomes, careers and pensions were at stake in the decision.[8]

In the 1970s when the decline in bed-days required the hospital plant of the Twin Cities area to be reduced, some very difficult decisions were made to merge institutions and to reduce bed capacity. Those principally involved were the chairs of the Minneapolis area hospital boards, citizen volunteers rather than salaried administrators. Those decisions would never have emerged from a discussion just among the professional hospital administrators. (When the trustees began meeting the administrators were in fact asked politely not to attend.)

The K-12 institution is not built like this, does not operate like this. The chair of the board is not, like a mayor, directly elected. Board chairs do not meet alone together to consider problems of the system and to develop proposals for their solution. Boards typically do not have staff of their own. District boards of education are sometimes trained even by their own associations to leave decisions to their superintendents: in the old phrase, to "select 'em and protect 'em".

The institutional weakness of the boards, the domination of the K-12 institution by the career professionals, severely constrains the ability of the policy bodies in K-12 to raise and resolve its most fundamental strategic problems.

---

[7]*Facing the Challenges of Whole-school Reform*, Berends, Bodilly and Kirby, RAND, 2002

[8]Ray Olsen, city manager in Bloomington, was a notable exception.

■ *Nor can superintendents lead on system change*

Is it possible then that the superintendents, closest to the changing situation and see-ing up close the need for change, might lead — if not personally then at least through their state association? In some public institutions these associations do work effec-tively on the system-problems of the institution.

This is unlikely. A case in Minnesota is instructive.

In the spring of 1998 Superintendent Don Helmstetter, in his year as president of the Minnesota Association of School Administrators (MASA), took an important initiative. He and a few other like-minded superintendents saw the implications of the state setting standards, introducing testing and unbundling K-12 in ways that permit public bodies other than districts to offer public education. Out of a series of late-afternoon and over-dinner meetings they developed an 'Agenda' for their state association to take to the Legislature.

Their Agenda proposed to put the strategic issue clearly to the Legislature: If you're serious about kids having to learn you need to be equally serious about giv-ing us the capacity to do that job. Our districts will accept these challenges from the state — even choice — if the state will in return give us real flexibility with people and with time, and the ability to control costs (including the ability to go to contract for learning programs). They said: "It is time to risk deregulation." They hoped their association would carry this message.

What happened is both enlightening and depressing.

The proposal never reached the Legislature. MASA, though polite to its (outgo-ing) president, was essentially uninterested. And the Minnesota School Boards Asso-ciation paid even less attention when the Agenda was presented to its state meeting by Tom Nelson, then the superintendent in Buffalo and a former commissioner of education.

Without association support the Agenda died.

We exaggerate what those in positions of leadership can do within present arrangements. Over and over, communities drop a superintendent and then imme-diately rush out to search for another, convinced the next person will be The Great Leader Who Will Turn Our District Around. The idea is of course encouraged by the candidates for the job: These are prestigious and well-paid jobs and people will make the promises they need to make to get them.

Unrealistic expectations of what 'the leader' can accomplish keep the public from seeing that, as the district is presently arranged, dramatic changes are impossi-ble to achieve no matter who is superintendent. And what is true at the district level is true also at the state association level. Helmstetter's initiative was an unusual act of leadership. But it failed. Under present arrangements the cards are stacked against leadership as well as against innovation.

Change is now an ethical question

How to respond to the pressure for change is becoming more and more an ethical question for the K-12 leadership. The traditional approaches to improvement are not working very well. Those inside know this. They need to say it, so the country can broaden its theory of action.

The realities are closing in rapidly on the institution. Student performance is measured and reported. The levels of learning and the racial and socio-economic disparities are a growing embarrassment. The country wants improvement. The institution clearly cannot reform itself enough, fast enough. It is exhausting legislators' patience with its plea for more time and its promises to do better. Year by year, standing pat and endlessly saying 'No' to significant change in existing processes and in the structure of the institution becomes less defensible. If it were true in 1986 that "We do have the option to stonewall it", it isn't any longer.

There is a major move the district leadership could make.

At the moment it resists the creation of new schools, the expansion of choic/es, because it cannot adapt its own institution to make its schools appealing to families now free to choose. Yet the states almost certainly would agree to increase the districts' capacity to change and to succeed if the district sector would accept the importance of the state creating also an open sector outside it.

The leadership of the institution needs to find a way to think about this, in its own interest as well as in the public interest. The transition to being 'an education board', overseeing schools run by others (including teachers) would be a radical change in traditional arrangements—even in the theory of public education. But realistically the leadership must consider also what will happen if it does try to stand pat.

Both the practical and the ethical questions come to focus on the boards. To a point the administrators and the union leadership can be allowed their resistance: Their members do have their professional careers and their personal finances directly at stake. It is harder to excuse the boards, whose members do not have the same private career and economic interests at stake.

The boards' real job is to represent the public. Over the years of running the schools the boards have come to think like operators, defending and protecting existing arrangements. Perhaps the greatest sadness in the whole discussion about improving education is to see the boards on the wrong side of the policy debate, not standing with the people, not fighting for the public interest and for the students.

Are there a few courageous individuals?

There must be some prospect that at some point some leadership will appear within public education to say: "We do have to move". It is unlikely to come from those commonly called leaders. To preside over an association is not necessarily to be a leader for change. Leadership for real change is more likely to come from those not in 'positions of leadership'.

It would not require everyone. A few well-placed individuals would be enough. A few superintendents, perhaps some board members, even union local presidents. Separately, or working together. At local, state and national levels. People currently working and people who have retired. "Six committed people can accomplish almost anything," Al Quie, the former governor of Minnesota, and a member of the commission that produced *A Nation at Risk*, likes to say.

Such an initiative would require explaining carefully the need now for strategic acquiescence. It would involve building a coalition, testifying to the legislature; making speeches, having informal talks. Perhaps generating a book. Meeting with newspaper reporters doing radio and television talk shows. The media would listen, given the unusual combination of the message and the messenger. It should not take long: Five years, perhaps less.

What about the teacher unions?

It has been common to blame the teacher unions for the inability of the districts to change and improve public education. The unions control the boards and the political process in which board members are elected, it is said; they will not accept accountability, will not accept changes that threaten teachers' individual and collective interests. This becomes an excuse for 'management' not succeeding with its effort at improvement.

But it is worth considering whether the behavior of the teacher unions, like the behavior of the boards and superintendents, might be a function of the incentive-structure we now have for K-12 public education. Teachers are salaried civil servants working for administrators, employed by an organization guaranteed its customers and its financing by virtue of its exclusive franchise to offer public education in the community. How can anyone be surprised that teachers unionize and that their union then takes advantage of the opportunities the public-utility arrangement offers to it?

This reminds us that an effort that accepts the traditional system arrangement accepts the constraints that go with it. It really is quite strange for those advocating improvement to complain about the unions and yet to insist that the effort at improvement must be held within existing arrangements. Yet it happens. Superintendents complain about bargaining, for example. But in most states if you are a public-sector employer you will do bargaining. It seldom occurs to district officials to think about not being an employer.

Given the difficulty of changing the district institution, one logical course for state policy leadership is to leave that sector of public education in its present form. Teachers in districts could continue in the present arrangements if they wish. Many parents are happy in present arrangements. The energy of governors and legislators could then be put into creating and enlarging the new sector of K-12 set up on different arrangements, with a different incentive-structure for teachers as well as for others.

Quite possibly the organized teachers would work to block state policy from moving this latter direction. But they have been opposed ever since the charter idea first appeared. And their efforts have been only marginally successful: Governors and legislators have proved willing and able to set in motion an unbundling of K-12 which now has significant strength and support and is proceeding fairly steadily.

It is possible the resistance will increase to the point where it threatens to stop or to roll back the effort made by state policy leadership. If so, then the burden of leadership will fall on others outside the institution who are concerned about public education, who see the dead-end at which the institution has arrived and who see the way out.

■ ■ ■ ■ ■ ■

Chapter **13**

IF THE LEADERSHIP JOB FALLS TO THE COMMUNITY

The communities that will improve fastest will be those that push hardest, that are most clear-headed about what really will work and that have the courage to move outside the district framework even against the wishes of those who run the districts. This will not be easy. But it can be done. It has been done. State policy leadership will act if it gets a clear and strong signal from these communities.

So the critical actors may in the end be those involved in the education-policy discussion outside K-12: citizens, business executives, foundation officials, newspaper reporters and editorial writers, and all those in the groups that work with children. Plus those who run the cities and whose success depends on the city being a place where families that need public education choose to live. It would be helpful, too, if students were at last given a voice in the decisions.

This leadership from the community can be decisive. Those inside K-12 have counted on unquestioning support from its major institutions. They will look to see if that continues. If it does, if no one signals it is time to change, then those inside K-12 who would like to change will be undercut and those who hope to stand pat will be reinforced. But if the public sends a strong message that, yes, it is time for the old public-utility arrangement to change, it will empower state policy leadership in absolutely critical ways.

The decision ought not to be difficult for those outside: They are not themselves vested in the existing arrangements. Yet it will be hard. The kids doing well are visible. The kids not doing well are out of sight. Traditional arrangements have a strong hold on almost everyone. Most people think of the district schools as the public schools. Most went to, sent their children to, these schools. Some have themselves taught or served on boards of education. Most of those in the discussion liked school as they knew it, and hope that somehow it can be better without having to be different. All this encourages people to think the problem must be the students and that the solution is to get tough, to make 'em learn.

It will be a big job to get the community leadership to see that we have a system problem, a problem in institutional design: good people, students and teachers, caught in a bad system that needs to be changed. It will not be easy to develop an understanding that change means more than firing the superintendent, throwing out the present board of education, passing an excess-levy referendum or raising standards. It will mean coming to appreciate that a new set of incentives will be needed, both to change the schools we have and to open up the opportunity for others to start different and better schools new. In this it will be all right to be radical, to be angry.

Gradually the discussion will become less naïve about what management can do in a static arrangement, more realistic about the limitations of trying to 'do' improvement and about the need to create a 'have to' for the organization. A concern for saving the kids will grow and the concern for 'saving the system' will fade.

Coming to this new view will be easier for some community groups than for others. Through the transition some people will be more reliable supporters than others. And leaders in the different sectors will need to play some new and different roles.

City Hall is a party at interest
It should be clear to those running large cities that their own hopes turn on whether or not their city is seen as a place where families that need public education want to live.

People who have choices are unlikely to remain in and are unlikely to move into neighborhoods where they cannot feel their children will get a safe and quality education. So all those involved with the future of the cities—mayors and city councils and downtown councils and property owners and neighborhood improvement organizations and community foundations and local employers and non-profit cultural institutions—are parties at interest in this debate about how to get quality schools. Their help will be needed in the effort now for system change and for the effort to start schools.

Until fairly recently cities and city officials were not heavily involved. When in the fall of 2001 the president of the Minneapolis City Council spoke on "major challenges facing the city", the schools—despite Minneapolis' startlingly low graduation rates—did not appear on her list. "Why not?" someone asked. "Not our job", she said.

Her comment reflected the separation of education from municipal government in most of the country. West of a line somewhere between Cleveland and Chicago is the land of the independent school district. To the east and especially in the old colonial states education is dependent; north of the Mason/Dixon line, an extension of town or municipal government and to the south, of county government. But even the dependent districts today are effectively beyond the reach of city leadership. In Rochester, N.Y., the president of the Urban League, Bill Johnson, ran for mayor thinking this would give him leverage on the schools. When elected he found how limited the mayor's ability is, to make the district move.

For years the temptation for city officials was to say the schools were, literally, not their job; that they did not know the institution, had no idea themselves how to cause improvement. They were sometimes irritated to be blamed for tax increases voted by the board of education. But a fight with the board was a fight the mayor might lose. It was better to stay out. So the schools operated independently. 'Schools' appeared in the city plan mainly in terms of what their location implied for city streets and parks. Improving the quality of education was not a part of the city's development program.

This proved unwise. Poor schools were increasingly making problems for the city. Bad education had bad consequences. Clearly the city government needed to do something. Following Mayor Harold Washington's initiative in Chicago in 1987 mayors began to get active. For some the answer was to take over the schools, as mayors did later in Chicago, Detroit, Cleveland, and elsewhere. This may or not may work: The jury is still out on takeover.

Others believe they get more leverage by working with the state to change the arrangements for public education in the city. John Norquist in Milwaukee was one of these; a mayor who worked with the state for changed arrangements, at times resisting the governor's effort to push him into takeover. Norquist helped the reform coalition in Milwaukee go to the state for charter and voucher laws that would generate outside pressure on the district, then worked to help the coalition get control of the board of education to generate a positive inside response.

The reform coalition in Milwaukee is always at risk, every election. Its members, at times holding a majority on the board, see the outside pressure as essential: Only when faced with the loss of jobs, they understand, does the district organization respond to the board's leadership for change. Few boards or communities are as politically sophisticated. It has made Milwaukee perhaps the most important site in America for education policy, largely unappreciated by national media that have so hard a time seeing beyond the controversy over vouchers.

One hopeful development is CEOs for Cities, a national organization formed largely by Paul Grogan at the Boston Community Foundation. It brings together the heads, the "CEOs", of business firms, colleges and universities, large medical institutions, community foundations, major arts and cultural organizations, and of the municipal governments. Its members understand that it will be impossible to build the city if they cannot offer good public education. Quickly the organization moved to the question of method. At its meetings in Chicago in late 2003 and early 2004 it was thinking beyond helping the superintendent and beyond mayoral takeover, to a strategy of new schools and new entities to create new schools.

Business needs to think strategically

Where the business community comes down can often be decisive in a debate about public education. Unhappily the big firms most prominently involved, and their chief executives, too often let themselves be coopted by the interest groups into a strategy of incremental reform, into the belief that the country can get the improvement it needs just by changing existing schools.

Because business influence carries such weight it is important that its leadership think clearly and independently about the problem of change and improvement. If business is to be effective in reshaping public education it will need to think strategically. Four things stand as challenges.

▨ The lure of reform . . . of change through 'leadership'

The importance of its support naturally makes the business community a prime target for lobbying by the education interest-groups. They know that business is decisive in many local decisions and in much of the state and national policy debate. They have become skilled at influencing the business leadership; of talking CEOs out of using their common sense. They say to the CEOs, in effect: You're practical people. Look: All the reform programs together don't enroll more than a handful of students. Ninety-five per cent of the students are in the district schools. The districts are where the job has got to be done. We're the ones who run the districts. You can't get things done working against us. Work with us.

No business executive wants to be thought 'not practical'. So in no time the CEOs are subtly steered away from the discussion about arrangements that the institution wants to avoid, and especially away from choice and from the state's effort to create schools new. In agreeing to work with the district the CEOs fall into the notion that the job can be done within existing arrangements, and agree to move only as far and as fast as the K-12 leadership itself is willing to move. Which is: not very. Business thus gives away its leverage.

It may seem surprising that experienced individuals would do this. There are several explanations.

Business people are susceptible partly because in truth the interest of top businesspeople in education is not as strong as it is usually made out to be. Listen, for example, to a CEO in Minneapolis—an individual more than ordinarily involved in politics and civic affairs—responding when sounded out about coming into the education-policy discussion:

> Let me tell you why it doesn't really make sense for a CEO to get deeply involved in this. First: You personally don't have a problem. By the time you get to this job your own kids are out of school. Or, if you have a late family, you can afford to live where you want or send your kids to private school. Second: This is not an issue you know. You don't feel you can impose your ideas. You wouldn't want somebody doing that to you, with your organization. Third: Reform is too controversial; takes too long. Fourth: Other things—taxes, regulation—really are more important. If you have a good company you don't have that much problem getting good employees. Finally: Business is just harder today. You have less time.

Business' public affairs has changed. Firms are larger now; have wider—even global—horizons. The local community is less important. Industry attention is focused less on the states; more on Washington. The public affairs departments once an extension of the CEO's personal office were in the '80s and '90s put to the service of the business. The mission of corporate giving and civic affairs is now to support the line units and the commercial objectives of the company.

CEOs are action-oriented people. Often they come into, or are brought into, public affairs to 'get things done'. Most do not see it as their job to explore the complexities of what ought to be done. They come in to sell a proposal. But they do not want to take on something they might lose, and fail in public. So they are cautious. Which makes them especially receptive, in the K-12 arena, to appeals from the district to "help us". This is safer.

Few CEOs would enjoy finding themselves on television, the superintendent jabbing a finger and saying, 'I'm trying to row this boat: Why are you trying to tip it over?' Controversy could have bad consequences for the business. Also, business people know that some in K-12 are prepared to play hardball if necessary. In the mid-1980s the heads of two Minnesota companies selling to the school market were warned that if the business community did not back off on its effort to "Cap State Spending" their businesses could be in serious trouble in the schools.

But beyond these personal and political explanations there is an even more basic reason why business people often do not think well when they enter the public arena to grapple with the problems in K-12 public education.

■ *Misperceiving a system problem as a management problem*

You might think that business people would bring to this policy area an understanding from their own experience of the systemic factors that require organizations to perform well and to change. But with some exceptions, often the people in technology firms, they do not. There are several reasons why they do not.

Business executives tend to be misled by their experience. Most of what they do and what they read and what they hear is about managing the organization. The titles on the Business shelf at the bookstore, the magazine articles, the lectures and conferences are all about how to steer the organization through the stormy seas; how to deliver quality, how to improve, how to change, how to survive. The literature takes as given the competitive environment in which business lives, accepts that because the risk of failure is real the organization must be continually improving, then advises leaders how to manage well.

This is of course the way the superintendent hopes business people will think when they come into public education. The tendency to focus on problems of management steers business people away from the important questions about the large-system-architecture of public education. It causes them to identify with the superintendent-as-CEO, which in turn causes them to defer to the expertise of those managing the district.

The suggestion sometimes heard, that business executives want to run the district, is probably mistaken. Superintendents who make this charge may just be trying to discourage any remaining impulse to interfere with district decisions. If so, that works. Business executives who persist in offering advice may be asked to 'Try being principal in my high school for a day'. The district knows how to build sympathy for the people in the schools.[1]

Business executives let themselves be persuaded that education is different. "If you bring me an insurance problem," I heard the CEO of a life insurance company say at one point, "I can talk with authority about that. I know insurance. I don't know education. I need the superintendent to tell me what the problems are. Then if I can help, I will." Not surprisingly many business executives find they prefer involvement as partnerships, adopting-a-school, supporting the superintendent.[2]

Business executives could make a far more important contribution than this. The K-12 leadership likes to say, as the Minnesota School Boards Association leadership

---

[1] At a Saint Paul Chamber of Commerce briefing on the schools I heard an administrator from a 1,600-student K-6 school explain in graphic detail how tough the job is where he works. In the discussion period he was asked a question he perhaps did not expect: "If you ran the district would you have a school that large in a low-income neighborhood like that?" "No, of course not", he said.

[2] David Kearns, chairman of Xerox Corp., was an exception. He was critical of "feel good" partnerships for "reinforcing the status quo". See his speech to the Economic Club of Detroit, October 1987.

once said fairly directly to the chair of the Minnesota Business Partnership's education task force: We know more about education than you do. A business executive like this one (in the health-care field) could quite properly say in response: Yes, but I know more about system change than you do. And that would be true. But this sense of competence is lost when executives fall into the notion that the problem in education is a problem in the management of the organization rather than a problem in the structuring of the industry.

It remains unclear why more business people do not see what is so obvious. In well-designed institutions with well-structured incentives the organizations themselves do the good things that are necessary: They set standards, measure performance, impose consequences, modernize technology, control costs, train leadership, plan succession and treat employees and customers well. If the organizations in K-12 do not do these good things themselves then probably the institution is not well designed and its incentive system is not well structured. The sensible course for business, then, is to get the system arrangements for public education set right.[3]

Unfortunately, business has too often not thought strategically; has not tried to find what was causing these good things not to be done and worked to fix that. It has gone along easily with proposals for the state to set the standards, introduce the measurement of performance and impose the consequences: gone into 'doing improvement' and into supporting what Arthur Wise condemned 20 years ago as 'legislated learning', "the bureaucratization of the classroom". By the time of the first presidential summit of governors and CEOs in 1989 big business, especially, had become a strong backer of the accountability model and an active proponent of legislation in the states to set up large and complex processes intended to drive into the institution the better practices the districts had not introduced themselves.

It will not be easy to get business to rethink its recent strategy. People can go on only one crusade at a time. Committed to master-planning as the method for improvement, the corporate leadership has not really been open to strategies that contemplated changing existing arrangements. This was confirmed in the subsequent summits convened by President Bill Clinton and by President George W. Bush. In these discussions choice, chartering and vouchers were dismissed as 'things the states might consider'; clearly not central and certainly not a substitute for the central effort to set standards, measure performance and enforce accountability; to transform existing schools.

---

[3]See "Education That Works: The Right Role for Business", Ted Kolderie, *Harvard Business Review*, September-October 1987.

■ *Getting involved in the wrong negotiation*

Business people often make the mistake of letting themselves be drawn into a negotiation in which district officials ask for more resources and offer better student performance in return.

Negotiating for improvement in education is not like buying a property, where
you hand the seller a check and the seller hands you the deed. The board or superintendent, or the association leadership at the state level, cannot hand you improved
student performance now. Improvement takes time. So when you push money
across the table they give you back an IOU, a promise of improvement later. And
there is no insurance, no surety bond.

In 1987 Rochester, N.Y., agreed to a contract that provided large increases in
teacher salaries in return for promises of change and improvement by the teachers
in the schools. The increases were put into effect right away. Three years later when
the contract came up for renewal the changes had not been made. The superintendent could not then agree to another round of increases, which the union president, Adam Urbanski, could not then fail to demand. Bad scene.[4]

Never, never bargain for 'improved student performance'. Identify changes that
can be expected to lead to better learning (or cost-control, or whatever other objective you seek). Insist on meaningful changes that the board will implement before
the levy increase is approved. Or if the question involves an increase in state financing, make your support conditional on the K-12 leadership having joined a successful effort first to enact the changes needed; then approve the appropriation.

■ *'Getting involved' . . . to help the company*

Sometimes a CEO gets involved in education for reasons that are neither personal
nor civic but that mainly have to do with the interests of the company itself.

Some businesses have K-12 as a major market. They sell products or services to
districts. Others have public-relations problems with their own business and want to
create a more positive public image. Not surprisingly the advisors in both cases often
think it would be good for the CEO to be seen positively involved with public
education.

Firms with these interests are willing to spend time and money in this area. But
inevitably their participation is constrained and constraining. Their business interest discourages them from giving support to any radical rearrangement that would
offend important groups. Better to avoid controversy. Stay tight with what the K-12
leadership itself favors. Try to be helpful.

---

[4]A year or so later, in a discussion in Minnesota, Albert Shanker was asked about this. "I told Urbanski
not to put the money up front", he said.

Unhappily, executives with these interests are often the most available when a business association is looking for someone to chair its education committee. The appointment then constrains the position of the association itself on questions about system-change. Sometimes the professional staff of the association can offset this influence, perhaps by adding disinterested members for balance. But a chairman with this kind of conflict can be a real challenge for the association. A big contributor carries a lot of weight.

Business executives ought to be sensitive enough to the public interest to resist letting the interests of the firm intrude into the policy debate about education. And business associations ought to keep themselves free to engage the central questions in this policy debate on the merits; should be careful not to be used for the private purposes of an individual member. Easier said than done, clearly.

Where firms and their executives cannot afford the controversy bound to accompany an effort to press public education to change, the best course may be simply to stay out, to move their public involvement to other areas. Again, easier said than done.

Some foundations are helping significantly

Private philanthropy has been helpful—critical, really—in supporting the implementation of the states' new strategy. The charter laws provided the authority and set up the process for creating the new schools. But the states were slow to provide adequate financing for school operations and especially for facilities. Giving filled the gap.

There has been a wide variety of donors involved; local and national, small and large. The support has not come notably from the larger and older national foundations, which remain generally committed to district action and generally in their traditional role of financing programs and projects on the cutting edge of conventional thinking.

Discouraged by the lack of results, some older foundations have been getting out; quietly in most cases, though the board of the Edna McConnell Clark Foundation and in 2002 three local foundations in Pittsburgh said publicly what they were doing and why. The Pew Trusts, for years a major source of financing for district restructuring, is now focusing its efforts on early-childhood education.

When approached by the district for support foundation executives should ask tough questions. Ask the superintendent: Is what you plan to do important? If the answer is 'Yes' then ask: Is it very important? If the superintendent again says 'Yes', then ask: Is it very, very important? If the superintendent continues to say how important the project is for the district then say: "Now tell me why it isn't important enough for the district to pay for itself".

It's fair to conclude that what a district isn't willing to pay for itself it does not really consider very important. And fair to conclude that something the district does consider important it will find a way to pay for itself. If there really are very important things that the district really cannot make a priority, then clearly something much more fundamental is wrong and the foundation should turn its attention to fixing that.

It is foolish, it sends all the wrong messages, to give money for things the district should be paying for itself. Far more that is far more lasting would be accomplished by changing system incentives in ways that would cause the district to make sure that the most important things are in fact financed and carried out.

Some of the newer (and often not small) foundations understand best the need to introduce dynamics, to make education a self-improving institution. These have been significant backers of efforts to change system arrangements to develop the new charter sector and to introduce new programs of choice in one form or another. The Walton Family Foundation was in early. Since the mid-'90s the Bill & Melinda Gates Foundation has been increasingly important, putting financing both into creating small new schools and—almost always through local non-profit intermediaries—into breaking-down large district high schools.

Foundations are right not to want to go on indefinitely financing improvements that do not last and do not spread. But it would be a strategic error for foundations to withdraw from the effort to improve public education. They should stay in, with a strategy that will be effective. They should get into the 'system' discussion.

They can do that. They do not need to lobby—though charitable funds can be used in limited ways to influence legislation. They can finance the design of new programs and new arrangements. They can help with the effort to educate the public to the understanding that public education is now more than the district. They can help finance a lawsuit or defend against a lawsuit.

Philanthropy has made a major contribution to the effort to create the needed capacity for change in public education.

We need the media to cover policy

Major institutional changes in this country usually require a serious policy debate. Traditionally the press has been a principal medium for this debate. The public needs to be educated about (whatever) problem and about the merits of various proposed solutions. It is important to have this discussion about the community's problems and what should be done about them. A sophisticated discussion about why things work the way they do and about how to change what causes things to work the way they do is a requisite for any successful effort to change system arrangements.

This was not easy in the best of times. In a real sense it is reporting for insiders. It requires an ownership that cares about solving fundamental community problems. But, unhappily, the publisher has no formal obligation to care whether public problems are solved or not.[5] And the reporters and editorial writers may or may not have a real understanding of the subjects they cover. Some reporters arrive knowing the field, but many rely on those in the field to tell them how the institution works. Knowledge of the subject is not required: No concept of 'certification' operates in this professional field.

And these are not great times for local newspapers. Television has taken much of their readership and they live in fear of what the Internet and the web might do to their classified advertising. With the business under pressure the newspaper cannot afford the close coverage it formerly gave to the community's public affairs. Editors today cannot justify having reporters living on beats, knowing and reporting the institutions and issues of public life in depth as they did in the past, telling people in a policy field what others in that field are doing and saying. Nor are local affairs any longer of prime interest to owners now increasingly headquartered elsewhere. Not very many people would, really, be interested. The person fascinated by policy, editors figure, will buy the paper anyway.

Newspapers today are trying to reach the occasional reader. So the coverage is changing. The focus today is on 'You'. The prosperity that followed World War II broke down what Daniel Yankelovich called 'the ethic of self-denial'. A new 'ethic of self-fulfillment' spread from college students to other youth and then to their parents. Quickly the newspapers moved to serve this new interest in your health, your career, your home, your entertainment, your recreation, your technology, your family. Newspapers, searching for readers, are now focusing on 'You'.[6]

This has seriously impacted the coverage of public affairs. In the 1970s the massive decline of public confidence in institutions reinforced this interest in private affairs over public affairs and gave the papers a way to explain why they should not be doing what they could no longer afford to do anyway. They moved dramatically away from covering governmental debates. The coverage of government became more about how what 'they' are doing affects 'you'. Partly it is about how public action might hurt you. Partly it is about how public action might help you. It means

---

[5]"A newspaper is a private enterprise, owing nothing to the public which grants it no franchise", a *Wall Street Journal* editorial said in 1925. When I joined the *Minneapolis Star and Tribune* the publisher had an explicit concept of the newspaper as an educational institution and of the reporter as the equivalent of a college professor. But that was exceptional.

[6]Expect even more that is personally-relevant and people-centered, more feature treatment, more about health, home, food, fashion and travel, more that shows you Things Are Working. For the full picture go to **www.readership.org**.

covering the daily operations of government that affect citizens directly: school openings, school closings, the appointment of new principals and superintendents, the annual budget and the periodic excess-levy referenda, campaigns for the school board, the yearly sign-up for school choice, the annual report on students' scores and the stories about interesting student activities. There are many veteran reporters who dislike these trends and try to maintain the old notions of coverage. But the times are against them.

It is hard to justify close coverage of the discussion about policy, and especially of the debate about system change. The system incentives and the institutional arrangements determine the way the district and the institution operate. But the discussion about changing arrangements affects the public only indirectly. It seems remote. It is complicated. Covering policy, anyway, produces mostly talk. Television never did like talk: Public-affairs programs, producers whisper to each other, are "radio shows with pictures". Now newspapers are coming to the same view. "Let me know when something happens," editors tell reporters. "We don't do 'process' stories", they tell the public. Also, in policy controversies it is hard to know whom to believe. This difficulty affects coverage. It can be risky to believe the critics. It is safe to believe the district officials. So a lot that is said by those in authority gets accepted at face value.

All these changes in reporting create serious problems for policy. Public affairs, especially policy, is talk; is what happens before the vote is taken. Where that talk is no longer covered, seriously and with deep understanding, something fundamental has changed in the processes of our public life.

When the news changes it will get reported

When events change the public's attitude, however, the reporting will follow. Chicago in 1987 is an important case. When the Chicago Teachers Union struck that fall for the ninth consecutive time the *Chicago Tribune*'s veteran schools reporter, Casey Banas, wrote a remarkable piece. It went well beyond what a reporter would normally write in the news pages. And it hardly provided a practical program for action. But it stands as an honest expression of long-suppressed frustration, an example of what journalists can do.

> The Chicago public schools need a complete overhaul. The 11-member board of education must be scrapped. The superintendent of schools must go. The striking teachers must be locked out. . . When the overhaul is finished there should be no board of education, no superintendent of schools, no bureaucracy, no teachers union. . . A radical problem cries out for a radical solution. The current stalemate offers a very rare opportunity to scrap the entire Chicago public school system and start over.[7]

---

[7]*Chicago Tribune*, September 20, 1987.

Mayor Harold Washington called a summit meeting that fall. The solution chosen was decentralization; schools with elected local councils empowered to appoint the principal and to adopt the learning plan. All understood this would take state legislation. A coalition of neighborhood and citywide leadership lobbied a bill through the Legislature in 1988 over the protests of the board, the superintendent and the union. It was a significant change in traditional arrangements.

In this Chicago's two major newspapers were active and important. The *Tribune*'s series was reprinted as *Chicago Schools: 'Worst in America'* (picking up the comment of former Secretary of Education William Bennett); the *Sun-Times*' Maribeth Vander Weele expanded her series, "Schools in Ruins", into *Reclaiming Our Schools: The Struggle for Chicago School Reform*, published by Loyola University Press in 1994. Some progress was made. Unfortunately the next superintendent proved a centralist, which left Chicago halfway across the stream balanced on a slippery rock, trying to decentralize and to centralize at the same time. Six years later the Legislature (at his request, by most accounts) abolished the board of education and transferred control of the schools to Mayor Daley. In time Daley began using Illinois' weak chartering law aggressively, especially to get around the intransigence of the high schools.

It will not be easy to get most newspapers most places to be this angry, or to expend scarce resources reporting the debate about system change. Most of the time the media will be comfortable with the way things are. Not that this is new. It is a conservative institution. "My picture of the world was much the same as my readers'", Lincoln Steffens wrote in his *Autobiography*, thinking back to his reporting about 1902. "The reporter and editor must sincerely share the cultural ignorance (and) beliefs of their readers. You may beat the public to the news but not to the truth."

But if the community is aroused, the newspapers and even radio and television will respond and provide the coverage needed for policy action. A huge amount could be done by one enterprising reporter in a half page a day. There is also some hope in the new electronics, in the web and email. These low-cost formats eliminate some of the old obstacles to specialist coverage. With an electronic newsletter a single journalist can report in depth both for those interested in 'system' questions and for the newspaper's general editors. This is now beginning, with the information services offered by interest groups and by nonpartisan organizations. Already these are better reading, more informative, than most of the newspaper reporting. Most are just not yet local. One way or another, the policy discussion will get reported.[8]

But today it is best not to look to the media for leadership.

---

[8]It is fascinating to watch how, increasingly, stories refer readers to websites.

It is time to listen to the students

Finally: Let the students into the discussion. They will bring a candor and a sense of reality that will benefit the discussion. I heard Donald Fraser, when mayor of Minneapolis, say—astonishingly—to the medical professionals of University of Minnesota Hospitals: "If you will just listen to what your customers are telling you, you will be amazed how much you can learn". The same needs to be said now to the educator professionals.

Students' involvement is legitimate and is likely to be valuable. They know better than any parent what goes on in school. They can talk with authority about how well school is working for them; about what is interesting and what is not, about which of their teachers are trying hard and which are not. The students are parties at interest in questions about the future of school. To date the students' voice has been pretty much excluded (perhaps because of their candor). How often do you see students present when adults gather to talk about education? How often are they asked what they think; more important, what they care about and what they want for their education? Listening to what the kids think would help in a discussion that is far too much about adult opinion.

For some years Misti Snow ran the MindWorks project for the *StarTribune* in Minneapolis. "Over the last 13 years," she said to me in 1996, "I've read more than a half-million letters from students, first grade to 12th, and the picture painted by the kids has grown increasingly dark. Many adults either ignore or simply don't realize the complexities of children's lives today."

In the spring of 1993 Arthur Harkins in the University of Minnesota College of Education asked 750 students in Minneapolis schools, fourth through twelfth grade, to believe the new superintendent needed their ideas about what should be improved in the schools. They wrote him their suggestions. Harkins found that regardless of school or social class, students want the school, the teachers and the administrators to treat them respectfully. They want clean buildings and good food. "They want to be treated the way they're treated when they go into Target," Harkins said, "or into McDonalds." If they are, Harkins found, they will give back quality work and good effort, with good attitudes. Kids want to learn, he is convinced, and are ready for much more challenging experiences than we are giving them.[9]

The students' testimony might be the most important, most effective, testimony of all about the need for a radical change in the institution. The lives of young people have been changed dramatically over the last few decades. Many of the routes into the adult world, and upward in the economy, are effectively closed to those

[9]See "Who Should Adapt? Kids to School or School to Kids?", Ted Kolderie, on **www.EducationEvolving.org.**

without credentials and many occupational areas are fenced off by those currently employed in order to protect their own jobs and careers. To close off the routes to success other than through school, and then not to make school work for all kids, would truly confirm that young people are today the most discriminated-against class of people in our society.

■ ■ ■ ■ ■ ■
Prospects

THINGS THAT ARE NECESSARY TEND TO HAPPEN

It is, quite simply, necessary for the country to improve what young people know and are able to do. But it will not work to command the organizations in K-12 to do better. The institution needs to change, and to change it needs the capacity to change. So it is necessary to create this capacity; necessary for the states to transform K-12 into a self-improving institution by withdrawing the 'exclusive franchise' and by creating an open sector in which both the districts and other entities can create new schools.

This process will require taking account of certain realities that are now obvious. It is obvious the existing arrangement of public education does create obstacles to improvement. It is obvious that state policy leadership does not have to be constrained by existing arrangements. It is obvious that policy could make it possible to start schools new as well to change existing schools. It is obviously possible to create professional communities of teachers that exist legally, and for these collegial groups to be given responsibility for the success of the school or department. It is obvious that the information revolution represented by the Internet and the World Wide Web creates the potential to individualize and to personalize learning, and that this will make it necessary to change the old notion of 'instruction'.

Nothing is as encouraging as the fact that all these things are necessary. Things that are necessary tend to happen.

To do what is necessary we will need to expand the current theory of action. The effort that has bet all the chips on transforming existing schools is unlikely to work, however insistent the commands from the accountability model that schools and students perform. The standards and testing and sanctions can produce failure. By themselves they do not produce learning. Schools and districts unable to succeed and unwilling to fail are likely not to comply. This would produce a crisis. Already leadership is feeling pressure to back away from present requirements. We cannot afford the risk we would be taking if we continued with an effort only to command improvement, had that 'strategy' fail, and went into crisis.

To deal with such a crisis—or, better, to anticipate and to prevent it—state policy leadership needs to break out of present arrangements; needs to move aggressively to create an open sector in public education in which new entities are creating new schools that motivate students to work hard and to do well. These schools will need to be open to new technologies, open to the desire of students to individualize and to personalize their education, open to radically different uses of the year and the day and open at last to leadership roles for professional teachers.

To succeed with this effort state policy leadership will have to be clear why it will not be possible to get the schools we need just by changing the schools we have. And will need to be clear what, alternatively, to do.

The expanded strategy set out in this book will not win everyone's support. The unbundling and opening-up of the institution is, however, necessary. "The philosophy that concentrates on what is necessary," Jean Monnet wrote in his *Memoirs*, "is more realistic than one that takes account only of what is possible". Conventional wisdom says that politics is the art of the possible. But as someone else has said, politics is not the art of the possible: Almost anyone can do what is possible. Politics is the art of making possible what is necessary.

Action depends politically on the states, pushed by private institutions in each state and, hopefully, encouraged skillfully by the national government. This book has tried to be realistic about the ability even of the nonpolitical organizations—the media, the business community, the foundations—to challenge the conventional thinking about public education. But they are the best hope. Their leadership is necessary. In time they will do their civic duty. Again: Things that are necessary tend to happen.

The confidence that the states will act is reinforced by the awareness that the forces at work will sweep around the institution if it tries to resist. Forces this powerful cannot be contained by existing legislation. The courier services, when they appeared, were a clear violation of the statutes against the private carriage of the mail. Yet quickly the country decided the Postal Service would not be permitted to suppress a new and superior service that it was not itself prepared to provide.

It will be the same with education. Learning is not confined to school. Lots of young people learn on their own. They are free to learn on their own. Many now know how to be in touch directly with more resources for learning than school can provide through the traditional technology of textbook and teacher-talk. Other organizations can assess what the young people know and can do.[1] Students are free to take these tests. Colleges and businesses are free to accept the results as a basis for their decisions to admit and to employ. So there are now alternatives to school.

---

[1]The Educational Testing Service has a subsidiary—the Chauncey Group International—that specializes in certifying performance. Annual revenues are about $85 million. *New York Times*, January 14, 2003.

Young people can also boycott school. Legally they are required to attend, but if day after day they went out and sat on the lawn, or did not come or did not take the tests, what would adults do?[2]

If the forces now at work do simply go around the existing institution what results will meet neither our traditional definition of public education nor our traditional test of equity. It would widen disparities in our society and would surely change public education in ways that those inside K-12 would not approve. But that would not stop its happening. So considerations both of equity and of preserving public education now make it necessary to reshape the institution.

Those in state policy leadership are beginning to see the futility of trying to force improvement into the old public-utility model. That effort has all the weaknesses of any 'conduct' remedy, requiring endless energy to secure compliance from organizations that have neither sufficient reason to comply nor sufficient capacity to comply. Sensing this, state policy leadership has been developing a 'structural' remedy. Governors and legislatures are building into the K-12 institution incentives—reasons and opportunities—for organizations to act, in their own interest and on their own initiative and from their own resources, to put the students and the public first.

Legislators and governors may not say this; may not see it even: Policy is often more what people do than what they declare. But steadily state policy leadership is adjusting the system and modifying the institution to introduce those new reasons and new opportunities. They are evolving a mixed institution that will be a self-improving institution. It is the strategy not of doing improvement but of "getting the fundamentals right".[3]

The predictable resistance to the changes that are needed should not discourage state policy leadership in this effort. "Resistance is always proportional to the scale of the change being attempted . . . The progress of change can be measured by the intensity of the resistance."[4] There are powerful forces working also in support of change. The two may now be about evenly balanced. It may not take much to tip the balance. Once the transition begins the job for policy may not be as difficult as many have thought.

Implementing fully this new theory of action will take time. It will be difficult. But the states' interest and the public interest will override the districts' interest if the districts do not move. Things that are necessary do tend to happen.

---

[2]In a Chicago suburb not long ago the students, aware that the testing was more important to the district than to themselves, used this leverage to 'negotiate' with the administration certain improvements in parking and other policies.

[3]See page 8.

[4]*Memoirs*, Jean Monnet, Doubleday, 1978.